# BUILD

# BIBLE STUDY

—A BEGINNER'S GUIDE TO LEADING STUDY GROUPS—

ERIC HARMER

TO REBEKAH, ABIGAIL AND WESLEY,
WITH LOVE

*Eric Harmer*

# CONTENTS

# THE AIM OF THIS BOOK

There is a vast untapped resource in many of our churches; a resource that, were it released, it could revolutionize church life in the Western world and increase the effectiveness of evangelism beyond our wildest dreams. It could also produce well-discipled, well-taught Christians who understand their faith and its implications for our world. That resource is the membership of our churches.

Many local churches may verbally acknowledge belief in the doctrine of the 'priesthood of all believers', while retaining structures that make it virtually impossible for that doctrine to be applied. The minister (or pastor or vicar) does everything except, perhaps, teach Sunday school. This means that many churches cannot grow beyond their leader's abilities.

The aim of this book is to make a very small contribution towards reversing that trend. I hope it will equip and embolden 'ordinary' church members to see that they can lead Bible studies, house groups, evangelistic studies and even help their own families to grow in faith. It aims to show that small group and one-to-one studies are incredibly effective ways of evangelizing and discipling people.

This is not a theological tome, although inevitably theology is a part of leading studies. It is first and foremost a practical book that seeks to work through some of the questions a person might have before starting a study group. It is written out of many years of experience (and mistakes) that have shown me what a crucial part these small group studies can play in the life of a healthy church.

Although each chapter deals with a separate issue, the book is designed to be read as a whole, and for that reason it would be best to read it through once, even if your main interest is one particular area, such as evangelistic studies. It is a book that can be used by members of any church, and I have deliberately tried to avoid denominational assumptions about church structures and so on. It will primarily appeal to those who are from churches where Bible study would be seen as a priority, but if it helps some who have never considered Bible study to begin to do it then that would be even more encouraging.

# CHAPTER 1

# PRACTICAL POINTS WHEN STARTING A STUDY

The heavy door creaked open. He stood for a moment as his eyes adjusted to the gloom and then hesitantly made his way in. The building reminded him of a horror film he had seen as a child; it had that sort of spooky feel to it. It was cold in there—colder than he expected—and he shuddered involuntarily. At the far end, some distance away, he could see a light and a small group of people in a circle. They seemed to be sitting in silence, but no one had heard the door or noticed his arrival. They looked as if they were frozen, waiting for something or someone. 'I think I'll give this a miss,' he said to himself, quickly retreating to the creaky door. Back outside in the warm evening sunlight he felt better, safe again. As he walked to the nearby shops, he thought about how he had felt and firmly decided that Bible study just wasn't for him.

## SO YOU'RE THINKING ABOUT LEADING A BIBLE STUDY?

Good Bible studies, like most things in life, don't just happen. For a study group to be effective it needs first and foremost the blessing of God upon it. It also needs careful thought and planning at a human level. Good preparation cannot be a substitute for God's blessing but it can certainly play a part in ensuring that the greatest possible benefit is realized from the study.

Several key areas need to be thought about before the study group starts, which will greatly influence its success or lack of it. Many of these are obvious and 'practical' rather than 'spiritual', but they are important nonetheless. As the scenario described above shows, a question as basic as where the study will be held can determine whether some people come along or not.

## WHERE WILL THE STUDY GROUP MEET?

This is the first and most vital practical point that has to be decided in setting up any small group or one-to-one study. It needs careful thought because, certainly in the initial stages, people will judge the study more by the venue than by the content of the study. If the venue is too inappropriate as far as they are concerned, they will be distracted by its faults to such an extent that they are not likely to take in much about the study itself. They will begin to wish they had never come and will start to look for excuses to avoid future meetings. This can seem a very worldly, unspiritual sort of attitude, but to think this is to make two mistakes. First, our spiritual and physical lives are intertwined. The idea that they are totally separate comes from Greek philosophy—not the Bible. Second, if we are planning an evangelistic study and the people participating are not practising Christians, they will be influenced by factors that might have very little impact on established Christians, who are able to ignore the location and focus on the helpfulness of what is being said.

## IN THE CHURCH

The obvious location for a study in many people's minds is the church building. It seems the right place for something 'religious' like a Bible-based discussion. Non-Christians, who may feel that the church is a holy building, may see it as an appropriate setting for looking at the Bible. The church building may be well known and easy for people to find. Such a venue can also give the study credibility in the eyes of those attending. People from outside the Church may worry that they are not being taught 'properly' in a study group that meets in one person's home. It may be easier for those with an unbelieving family to go out rather than study in the home, where it could be a source of friction.

The facilities at a church can be useful. There may be a room that can used as a crèche or children's play area, perhaps already equipped with toys. This is vital if any of those coming to the study have children. It is simply not realistic to think that parents can amuse the children and get much out of the study, and you will need to arrange some sort of childcare facility while the study is going on. Either the members of the group can take it in turns to look after the children, or someone else from the church can be brought in to do it as part of their support for the study. This will encourage those with children to come, when otherwise they may have been fearful that the children would embarrass them or disrupt the study.

Care needs to be taken in deciding who will look after the children. Ideally it should be someone already involved in children's work in the church. It would not be advisable to let a complete stranger have sole charge of the children unless they were in sight of the study group. Your church should have a child protection policy and this must be made clear to all those who will be helping to care for the children, even if they are members of the study group but not the church.

Generally it does not work well to have the study during the day in school holidays, unless those coming have much older children or none at all. The resources of most crèches would be stretched if the age gap between the children ranged from 1 to 12. The presence of older children in the study would also tend to hinder discussion, especially of more personal matters, since children have an awful habit of repeating what they have heard to the least appropriate person! It would be better either to meet in the evenings during the school holidays, or just arrange a social event (to keep the group in contact with each other) which the children can also attend.

All of the above are good reasons to have the study at the church, *provided* the church building is suitable. Sadly, many churches are simply not, perhaps because of size, heating, state of repair and so on. A small group meeting in a church that seats several hundred can feel quite overwhelmed, which will have a negative effect on the group dynamics. Temperature can be another problem. Many churches were built before adequate heating systems were available. Nowadays people are used to centrally heated homes and find anywhere colder hard to tolerate. The same is true of seating. If the church has only fixed wooden pews that make one's anatomy ache after a few minutes, it will be very hard to generate a relaxed, informal atmosphere, and sitting in a circle would be awkward too!

Many churches were also built before the invention of the car and so have little or no parking space. Those in town centres can be particularly at a disadvantage since there may be no parking on a weekday for some distance around. Having to walk can be another obstacle for those thinking of attending. In an ideal world everyone would be so spiritually minded that they would think nothing of a 15-mile walk in the snow to study God's word, but we do not live in an ideal world!

Many churches have smaller rooms or vestries that could be available instead of the main church building. These can be better, but before you use them try to look round the room as if you were seeing it for the first time in order to assess its suitability. It may be that you are suffering with 'familiarity blindness', where you cease to see the dirt or discomfort. I have experienced this in my own home, where the DIY jobs that I meant to do when we first moved in were not done then and remain undone today. I have just got used to them! The same can happen in churches—one can proudly welcome a study candidate into a room we think suitable, only for the candidate to be horrified by the state of it, something we have become oblivious to. I remember visiting a church for the first time and noticing how all the paint on the end wall was blistering and peeling and covered with mould. It had obviously been like that for a long time, but the regular congregation did not notice. They had seen it so often that they didn't see it any more.

## IN THE HOME

An alternative to the church building is of course a home —either that of the study leader or of one of the people doing the study. There are a lot of advantages to holding the study in the home of a group member. First, it helps to ensure that they are there! One of the most frustrating aspects to leading a study is the irregular attendance of some of the group, and if it takes place in a home this will ensure at least that household's attendance.

Second, someone's home usually has a more relaxing atmosphere. There are none of the difficulties associated with church buildings, and the furniture and room size are more conducive to an informal approach. Relationships between group members seem to develop faster in a home meeting. The fact that one of them is sharing their home, and thereby part of their life, seems to open conversations at a more personal level and help to give the meeting more of a family atmosphere. If part of the study involves showing a video this is also usually much easier in someone's home. If it is an evangelistic study, it can help overcome the problem some non-Christians have with church buildings. This can take two forms: for some, simply entering a church building is a worrying thought (some people even think they might be haunted!) More common is the fear (especially in a small community) that someone they know will see them going in and will ask questions or express surprise that they have 'gone religious'. Going into someone's house can more easily be explained away.

However, there can also be difficulties with using someone's home. Catering for children can be a problem, since it may not be possible or appropriate to take the children to another room. And, as I've already mentioned, if the person is from a non-Christian home other family members may not like the idea of a study being held in their home. There can also be problems with pets. The host may have cats and one of the group may be allergic to them; or a dog may persistently interrupt the study wanting its owner's attention. Generally, though, these kinds of problems are easier to resolve than some of the problems associated with churches. (It's easier to put the dog in the garden than to take out the pews!)


## IN THE COMMUNITY CENTRE
## OR EVEN THE LOCAL PUB

A third option is to hire a neutral venue, such as a community centre, and there may be particular circumstances which make this a valid alternative. It would only be suitable for a larger group, however, and not for one-to-one or very small group studies. The cost may also be a drawback, since it would usually be the one leading the study who ends up paying for it, unless the church were willing to do so. Another disadvantage can be that of disturbance from other groups using the facilities at the same time. If the atmosphere is chaotic and noisy your group will find it hard to learn and ask questions The big advantage of such a venue is that it is a genuinely neutral location and some people might find it easier to study there than at either in a home or a church, both of which could be seen as someone else's territory.

Most pubs have a room that they make available for functions and these are sometimes free on the understanding that food and drink will be bought at or after the meeting. This can be a good venue for a men's group. A coffee morning in someone's lounge won't seem very manly to some! Men can often find it quite hard to talk about what they really feel and believe, and being in a place with other men can help them feel that what they are doing isn't quite so odd. They may then feel easier about inviting other men along as the study develops, since the pub is a familiar venue.

It is worth bearing in mind that one of the factors that has helped the Alpha course to be so successful is the great care it takes with details like the setting. Before your study starts, take time to think about who will be coming and which venue would best suit them. It may even be an idea to ask some of the group which sort of venue they would find most appropriate. Stay flexible, though, and if the first venue you choose becomes unsuitable for one reason or another be prepared to move.

The New Testament describes the early Church as

meeting in a range of venues. They didn't have church buildings as we would now understand them; instead the church usually met as part of the Jewish community in the synagogue or, if that wasn't possible, or if they were prevented from doing so, in someone's home (Acts 17:2–3; Acts 18:7). Occasionally they used a neutral public building (Acts 19:8–9). The early Church placed its emphasis much more on living as the community of the people of God rather than considering certain places 'holy'. Where they met was irrelevant compared to why they met.

## SPIRITUAL ISSUES

Why is the study group being set up? There are many possible positive reasons, but one major negative reason has to do with the question of motive. If the aim of the study is to create a 'church within a church' because the group is unhappy with the main church leadership, then the Lord is best served by the group not taking place. Its only outcome will be division within the body of Christ.

Another wrong motive could be pride. Some people like to view themselves as great preachers or gifted counsellors but have not yet found an opening in Christian work. This may be because the time has not been right, or it may be that they are simply not good enough or don't have the right temperament. To set up a group to ensure you have someone to dazzle with your preaching or emotionally heal with your counselling, rather than because you believe in what the group can achieve, shows a wrong motive.

A good question to ask yourself is whether you would be just as happy if the group was set up with someone else leading. If your answer is no, you need to look long and hard at your motives. Everyone needs to feel wanted, but there are some people in churches who seem to find their value and sense of self-worth only in the degree to which they are needed. Setting up a group of people who will become dependent on you and thus meet your inner need is wrong. Of course you should not end up desperately analysing your motives at every turn, but a degree of self-honesty is important at the outset.

## PRAYER

Make sure you set aside time for praying about the group and the study. You will have many decisions to make before the first study takes place and these decisions need to be made prayerfully, not just on the basis of what seems a good idea. Once the group is up and running it is important to keep praying. Pray for each member of the group individually. Don't underestimate the impact that Bible study can have on a person's life; and if there is ongoing prayer for them as well this can make a real difference. Pray that people will not be distracted from the message in some way, or prevented from attending the studies—this is especially important when it is an evangelistic study. Sometimes it seems that no sooner do people start a study than everything that can go wrong does and they are hindered from attending. There is a danger of focusing so much on the practical aspects, such as the venue, that you lose sight of the fact that this isn't just another meeting. If there is to be spiritual progress there must be prayer.

## PRAYER IN THE GROUP

This will depend on the group and people's expectations. Remember, you are running a Bible study group, not a prayer meeting. Certainly the studies should start with prayer and if in the course of the discussion a situation is mentioned which obviously calls for prayer then do stop and pray. It may be that one purpose of you setting up the study group is to show that there is need for a prayer group. You can do both if time is allowed for each so that neither gets squeezed out. In an evangelistic study it may well not be appropriate to pray, however. Non-Christians often feel very uncomfortable about prayer in a small setting and it could be a major factor in putting them off coming again. Once they have come to faith, and the group is effectively a discipleship course, then it would be important to begin introducing prayer as part of the learning process. Don't push people who are reluctant into praying out loud, and don't have long, embarrassing silences. Mention beforehand that silence can be an entirely appropriate aspect of prayer and this will prevent one or two feeling they have to 'keep it going' by endlessly and repetitiously praying about the same things.

## WHAT SORT OF PERSON LEADS A STUDY?

Far more people are capable of leading studies and leading them well than realize it. This is largely due to the fact that in the Western Church the tradition is to leave it all to the professionals, with the average member contributing little. Certain personality types will find it easier than others, however. Few people will be totally inappropriate, but some may have to work harder at it than others. It is important to be aware of your own strengths and weaknesses, and the input of an honest friend can help with this! Sometimes people are just not aware how talkative they are or how aggressively they come across. This can create problems in a study group. It really is important to know what sort of leader your personality is likely to make you and to guard against its excesses. Perhaps the most important thing is to be able to get on with all sorts of people. Simply being able to relate to people and make them feel at ease is incredibly helpful in setting the atmosphere of the study group. If the person leading the study seems tense and uncomfortable, then the rest of the group is probably going to feel that way. It is important to find the balance between a relaxed meeting and one that gets the study done. A laid-back meeting may be acceptable occasionally but if it happens too often the group members would get frustrated.

Generally, people fit into one of two personality types: confident and outgoing or shy and retiring—although most people are somewhere in between these extremes.

Each type will face different challenges in successfully leading a study—and knowing your own personality type is a crucial factor in the group, because the leader is the single greatest (human!) influence on the success or failure of the study.

The leader needs to be able to talk enough to keep the group going through those awful silences (especially at the start), but not talk so much that the rest of the group is excluded from any discussion. If you are a more dominant personality it may be useful to have a friend (or spouse) in the group who will tell you afterwards if you said too little or too much. It is vital that the discussion does not become a 'pulpit session' for a frustrated preacher, but rather a genuine interaction between the members of the group. The leader is there to facilitate discussion and give answers to questions that others wouldn't necessarily know. Often a dominant personality type will want the answers to the questions to be exact, and will have an almost overwhelming urge to correct anything that is said that appears even in the slightest part vague. That urge must be controlled! Obviously if the answer completely misses the point or is seriously heretical the leader should say something, but generally it is much more effective to try and get the group to think through what has been said and to clarify and sharpen the answer.

If you are a quieter person, the thought of keeping the group going through a silence may seem terrifying. It does become easier with time, but in the initial stages it may help your confidence to over-prepare—in other words, to have too many questions (many of them asking the same thing in different ways) so that if all the answers are monosyllables you will be able to keep going. Write the questions out, as memories can go cruelly blank under pressure, and keep the list discreetly in your Bible. If it still seems too daunting a task, there is no reason why you have to lead the study on your own. A married couple or two friends could act as co-leaders, easing the workload in terms of preparation and organization. It is probably not a good idea to have more than two leading since that can cause all sorts of communication problems.

## WHICH BIBLE VERSION DO I USE?

There is a very wide (and some would say confusing) range of Bible translations available in English today. Deciding which is the right version to use in your study group will depend on a range of factors. First, which version does your church use? While this may not be the decisive factor, it is a very important one. If the study is with non-Christians they can get very confused if the version they have learned to find their way around in the study is very different from the one they subsequently hear when they start attending church. Even for believers it can be awkward, especially if they remember a verse in one version and find that it is very differently phrased in another.

Second, what is the academic ability of the group? Some people find reading more difficult than others and can understand much more of what the Bible says if it is in easier English. Overall it is probably best to use a modern English translation rather than the King James Version (KJV). Some people (including some non-Christians) feel that the old English is somehow more holy and are almost superstitious about it. Some very real problems are created by its use today, however. First, many of the words used in the KJV have changed their meaning—for example 'conversation', which in 17th-century English meant lifestyle, rather than just talking to someone. Unless the study leader is aware of this and continually reminds the group of it, they will end up drawing misleading conclusions. The misuse of Jesus' words in Matthew 19:14 ('Suffer the little children') by Christians, as well as in society generally, is a good example of this. The old English word 'suffer' simply means 'let'. I have personally encountered non-Christians who interpret this verse as an indication that Jesus wants children to suffer!

Second, the KJV includes some translation errors that could cause problems for non-Christians in particular. For example, in Job 39:9 an animal is described as a unicorn. To have a mythical creature mentioned in the Bible might suggest that it is no more historical than a fairy story. Most recent translations use the words 'wild ox' which is much nearer to the sort of creature intended—and at least oxen aren't mythical. The KJV also refers to the use of steel (Psalm 18:34), hundreds of years before it was invented. This is in fact a mistranslation of the Hebrew word for hardened bronze, but a well-informed non-Christian is more likely to see it as a demonstration that the Bible is historically unreliable.

This is not a criticism of those who originally translated the KJV—they did an excellent job with very limited resources. Translators today have the benefit of several hundred years of additional archaeological research. It is also important to stress that the original manuscripts were not in error, but merely the translation of them into English.

While the parables of Jesus may be understandable in the KJV, the more complex theological passages, such as Romans, are very difficult indeed when read in 17th-century English. This may not be such a problem for well-taught, mature believers but for unbelievers and new Christians this could present a real barrier to grasping the concepts being presented. Some of them may simply give up, unable to understand any of it. It is difficult to see how it can be pleasing to the Lord to put unbelievers off the gospel by using a particular translation unnecessarily.

Old-fashioned language also reinforces the idea that the Christian faith is out of date, something that could be a real problem when trying to reach younger people with the gospel. Many people view Christianity as something appropriate for a more primitive age, and now that science has opened our minds to the reality of the universe around us, religion is out of date. Persistently using a Bible written in quaintly phrased Shakespearean English (however poetic it may be) does nothing to shake that impression. Some churches like to boast that they preach 'the old-fashioned gospel'. This is a ridiculous thing to say! The gospel—God's message of how a lost human race can be reconciled to him through the saving work of the Lord Jesus—can never be out of date. It is timeless and unchanging, but never old-fashioned.

A central teaching of the Reformation was that the Bible should be available in the common language of the people. It was the heroic efforts of early translators such as Wycliffe and Tyndale that enabled the people of that time to have the Bible in their own language and to learn its meaning for themselves, without having to rely on the priests. It is a tragic irony that some of the churches which claim to revere their memory insist on a Bible version that reverses the very thing they were trying to achieve.

Some of the key doctrines of the Christian faith are also clearer in the newer translations and this can be helpful when explaining these teachings to those who are unfamiliar with the faith. This is especially true of the doctrine of the divinity of Christ. Groups such as the Mormons and the Christadelphians like the KJV and use it because it is not explicit in its rendering of key verses such as Romans 9:5 and Titus 2:13 compared to translations such as the New International Version.

Sometimes people claim that the KJV is based on more reliable manuscripts (the so-called Received Text) than other translations. There is no real evidence that these manuscripts are more accurate than others, but if this is an issue for some then the New King James Version can be used, which is also translated from these manuscripts. This version follows the KJV but has corrected the translation errors (no unicorns!) and, being in modern English, is considerably easier to understand.

At the other extreme, be careful not to use a translation for study that is simply a paraphrase, as it can be difficult to examine in detail the words used. A paraphrase does not reflect the original wording to any literal extent. These very loose paraphrases (such as the Living Bible or *THE MESSAGE*) may be helpful for reading, but are probably not the best for a study. You will have problems if you are using a commentary or a Bible dictionary alongside a paraphrase since it won't have many of the words referred to by these books.

The other problem with a paraphrase is that it is only one interpretation of what the words mean. So instead of the group members themselves working through the meaning of the words, the paraphrase just tells them, and may not always be accurate or comprehensive. A word like 'justification' probably won't even appear in a paraphrase since its meaning will be given instead. But the doctrine of justification is far more complex than can be encapsulated in one line in a translation or paraphrase. It is better for the group to learn about the word, and its meaning and application, in the context of the meeting.

People may well turn up to the study with all sorts of versions (I have even known someone bring a Jehovah's Witness Bible along), so it might be helpful to have a few spare Bibles around in the version you are using to ensure that everyone is using the same version from the outset. This means that you can give out page numbers as well as biblical references, making it easier for those not familiar with the Bible to look up the right passage as quickly as everyone else. If you or the group cannot afford to buy the Bibles you may be able to borrow some from your church. Many churches today have pew

Bibles and it may be worth asking the church leadership if they could be borrowed for the study. This has the additional advantage that a new person to the church will already be a little familiar with that particular edition. Obviously none of this must detract from encouraging each person to have their own Bible and to read it between the studies.

## THE FIRST STUDY

Undoubtedly one of the most important studies for your group is the first one. Impressions formed then will take a long time to change, and if they are negative impressions you won't have an opportunity to change them, since your members may never come back! So you need to plan the first study very carefully. It will obviously be much easier if the group members already know each other, or if it is a one-to-one study. The hardest first study scenario is with a small group of people who do not know each other. They will feel awkward about talking and will be especially fearful of giving a 'wrong' answer and ending up looking stupid in front of everyone. Give time for the group to grow into the study slowly. One way to do this is to start the first session with a Christian video, followed by a short time of discussion. It is better for people to leave feeling they had more to say than for the meeting to drag on too long. Obviously it helps if there is some link between the video and the study! The availability of Christian videos is much better than it was and they cover quite a range of topics.

It would be worthwhile to visit each prospective member of the group before the studies begin so that you can begin to build a relationship with them and they will feel that they know at least one person there. You will also get a chance to assess how the various members will fit into the group. Look for the more confident ones, who could read aloud easily. Note those who are very shy, and who will need some encouragement to contribute to the group. Make a note not to put them on the spot in their first study—a sure way of guaranteeing they never come back!

Give careful thought to the question of who the study will be aimed at. Is it going to be a study for Christians or non-Christians? Sometimes people claim it is possible to cater for both but in reality this is rarely possible. Instead what often happens is that the focus of the meeting shifts slowly to favouring the believer and the seeker is (usually unintentionally) made to feel like an intruder on their discussion. If the reverse happens there is the very real possibility that the Christians will be put off because the issues being discussed and the ground covered may well be too basic. Lack of Bible knowledge would be another difficulty for a combined study as the non-Christian will probably not know the layout of the Bible and how verses and chapters work. You will need to give time to working through this, whereas it could of course be taken for granted in a study with established believers. This does not mean you have to ban all Christians from attending an evangelistic study. There are some real advantages to having one or two around at the study to help it along. They could for instance help in answering some of the questions, saving you from having to do it all. You could also encourage them to build relationships with the 'seekers' in the group, even meeting up at other times. Friendships formed in groups like these can be crucial to their effectiveness.

Decide what is to be the aim of the study. You may want to deal with issues of discipleship, such as prayer or giving, or choose a more in-depth examination of particular topics or books of the Bible. For the group to work well people need to know why they are there. It doesn't have to be an impressive-sounding or complicated aim—simply choosing the aim of encouraging believers in their faith is good enough. Or it could be an inter-church group, as there is no reason to assume that everyone will come from one church fellowship.

## HOW WILL YOU PUBLICIZE THE STUDY?

It is one thing to decide to hold a study but it is quite another to get anyone to turn up to it! You do need to think about the whole question of publicity. If it is to be an evangelistic, one-to-one study you will not need any publicity at all. If it is designed for a specific group of people from your church, again it is unlikely to need publicity. If, however, it is planned as a special interest study (see Chapter 5 on studies with believers) then you will need publicity. The most straightforward method is to produce is an A5 sheet giving details of the study, the venue, the time and so on. This can be photocopied and circulated at very little cost. Before sending out any publicity do check it out with your church leaders, since, if you have their support, other churches are more likely to feel happy about sending their members along. Make sure the publicity includes a contact phone number. This sounds obvious but it is the sort of thing people tend to overlook! Some churches may be willing to advertise it in their newsletter or magazine, but for them to do this you would have to contact their church leadership and reassure them that you are not sheep-stealing (trying to tempt their members to your church).

A major problem with publicity is that it often doesn't work. Churches are bombarded with information and advertising and one more piece of paper can easily get lost. Publicity can help extend the circle from which you draw group members but it would be best to have an initial core membership drawn from personal contacts first. If you are sending leaflets to other churches try phoning the minister first. This can introduce you, and it means that when the minister gets the publicity he or she will already know something about it and will have had an opportunity to ask questions and express any concerns.

## CHECK THAT ALL IS READY

Given overleaf is a checklist for you to use before your first study. It summarizes some of the information in this chapter and saves you re-reading the chapter half a dozen times in the run-up to the first study.

## CHECKLIST OF THINGS TO DO

1. Decide on a venue: church, home, neutral.
2. Why is the group happening?
3. Remember to pray about every aspect of setting up the group.
4. What study material will you use?
5. Which personality type are you?
6. Identify those you will invite, and invite them.
7. Which Bible version are you going to use?
8. Plan publicity, if appropriate, and think about contacting ministers of other local churches.

# CHAPTER 2

# BUT DO I KNOW ENOUGH?

All eyes in the group turned to look at Peter, the new study leader. Old Mr Alfred had done it again. He'd come up with one of his seemingly unanswerable questions. There was an awkward silence. 'Well, er...' said an obviously unsure Peter. 'I have to say I've never really thought of that. I suppose I don't know.' Mr Alfred looked smug and triumphant. Peter looked worried. Perhaps he shouldn't be a study leader after all.

One of the factors that puts many people off leading a study group is that they feel they don't know enough. Some Christians may relish the opportunity to display their knowledge to a gathered group and to be viewed as a guru, but many believers worry that they will be asked a question they cannot answer, or that they will look foolish as their lack of Bible knowledge is revealed. Obviously if someone is a new believer or really doesn't know anything, then they may need to take some time for their own study beforehand. Most Christians, though, are more competent than perhaps they realize. A wide range of resources is available that can help deepen knowledge and resolve some of the more knotty issues.

## HOW MUCH KNOWLEDGE IS ENOUGH?

Many groups can be lead using prepared study material so that much of the work is done for you. Some knowledge is still needed, however—first, to answer additional questions that arise from the study group, and second, to help illustrate and clarify the points the study is making. It is surprising what issues can come up, and while no one expects expert answers, some background knowledge is helpful.

First, you do need to know your way around the Bible, its overall story and roughly who appears where in the various books. This would not necessitate memorizing hundreds of verses but just the overall layout—knowing that King David appears in 1 and 2 Samuel, and Noah is in Genesis, and so on. You should be able to give a rough outline of the themes of each book of the Bible, even if you don't know them inside out. This requires nothing more than a little effort to read and note the central themes. A very helpful book for this sort of background knowledge is *The Handbook to the Bible*, published by Lion.

At the end of this chapter is a brief Bible knowledge quiz. It isn't the perfect way to assess yourself for suitability, but it might help highlight certain areas of Bible knowledge that you need to work on. A common problem is not knowing enough about the Old Testament. Some churches seem to preach and study almost exclusively from the New Testament, resulting in believers who have little idea who Amos was, let alone what he said.

This avoidance of the Old Testament can be for several reasons. Some people may think it has little relevance to church life, since it deals with the nation of Israel before the coming of Jesus. While it is true that some Old Testament laws and practices cannot be directly related to life today, we cannot truly understand the significance of Jesus' life, death and resurrection without understanding something of that first covenant with Israel. Also, many of the principles set out in the Old Testament do apply today and are reinforced in the New Testament. A helpful book on this whole area is *Living as the People of God* by Chris Wright (IVP, 1983).

Some people avoid the Old Testament because it seems to present a much harsher view of God than the New, with conquest and wars being used by the Lord to fulfil his purposes. But in fact some of the most moving passages about God's love for his people are found in the Old Testament (for example, Hosea 11), and some of the most terrifying imagery of judgment is found in the New (for example, Revelation 16). So don't be afraid of the Old Testament in your studies—it is part of the Bible!

You will also need a general grasp of theology. This certainly doesn't mean you have to go to theological college, but it could be helpful to know the different streams of thought in Christian theology and the way in which they use scripture. It is important to be able to put together a 'bigger picture' theologically showing the relationships between various denominations and beliefs. Many Christians are familiar with their own denomination's beliefs but can be surprisingly ignorant of other branches of the Christian Church, although it is important not to study them with the attitude of seeking to prove them wrong. No part of the Church has all its theology right and we can learn from other denominations.

You should have a basic understanding of church history. Many believers simply ignore this subject but it is actually quite important if the development of theology and the various denominations is to be put into any sort of meaningful context. The subject may be dismissed as boring by Christians, but if it was better understood some of the errors of the last hundred years could have been avoided. The teachings of groups like the Mormons and the Jehovah's Witnesses are not new —they had their counterparts in the first few centuries of church history. As with the other areas, you won't need a detailed knowledge, but an awareness of the church history time-line—who came when and what they did—would be fairly easy to acquire.

## USING BIBLE STUDY AIDS

There is a very wide range of Bible study aids available to help give some of the information you might need. Christians can be influenced by two unhelpful attitudes here: one is to say there is no need for any Bible study aid. Just pray, listen to the Lord and the meaning of the passage will be clear. And there are times when the Lord does reveal things to his people in this way and we can understand a passage of scripture without opening a commentary. The New Testament, however, puts great emphasis on being willing to accept godly teaching and gives little room for individual interpretations (see, for example, 1 Timothy 4:6; 2 Timothy 3:14; Hebrews 13:17).

The other extreme is to view Bible study as an academic exercise, where the exact meaning of the Hebrew and Greek must be teased out and hours given to doctrinal analysis. While this may thrill a certain sort of person, many will find that it has no relevance to their lives and personal situations, and it will exclude those who simply do not have the academic skills or background to join in the discussion. Talking about ideas that leave your life unchanged was an unknown concept in the New Testament Church. The assumption was always that believing something would have an impact on real life (see James 2:14–26; 1 John 3:17–18).

Unfortunately many of the most useful Bible study aids are not cheap, although some ministers are given a book allowance by their church to help with the cost. If buying a range of Bible study aids is beyond your means, you have several options: one would be to persuade your church to set up a reference library. This is worth doing even if you have all the books you want. A well-run (and promoted) church library could really encourage people to begin to study in greater depth and to take their Bible reading more seriously. You could also ask family and friends to give you some of these books as birthday and Christmas presents. This saves them the hassle of thinking what to get you and saves you getting any more unwanted socks! If you know other study leaders well you could arrange to buy the books between you and use them on a rotational basis. You may even find your minister is willing to lend you his or her books. Charity shops and second-hand bookshops can also be a good source.

## STUDY BIBLES

The simplest tool is a study Bible. This is a Bible with additional information about the historical setting of each book, some background information about the authors and a basic commentary on each page explaining what the text is about and drawing attention to any relevant information. Many of them also have cross-reference listings so that you can look up comparable texts on certain subjects They also usually have a list of major events in the Bible and where to find them. If you feel you don't know your Bible quite as well as you should or are afraid you just won't remember everything, a study Bible can be invaluable, although they can be quite expensive. Bear in mind, however, that many study Bibles have a denominational bias. The clue to this may be given in their title, such as *The Wesleyan Study Bible* or *The Spirit-Filled Life Bible*. It is probably best to get a general study Bible that will offer a range of views rather than one that reinforces what you thought anyway.

## USING A COMMENTARY

For those who want more detailed information about a particular book of the Bible, a commentary can be useful. This is a book which goes through a passage in detail, explaining what it means, how it fits into an over-all theology and giving some illustrations to help with the application of the verse to everyday life. These vary enormously from the very basic to those that assume you know Greek and Hebrew; and from modern editions to those that were written nearly five centuries ago. For someone without formal theological training the commentary series known as *The Bible Speaks Today* is very helpful (published by IVP). The *New International Commentary* series (published by Eerdmans) is also good. Although these are slightly more technical they still have a clear emphasis on the application of biblical themes to life. It is important not to think of commentaries as infallible. They are not scripture, but they can be a useful guide, especially with some of the knotty verses that really do not seem to make much sense. If your local Christian bookshop doesn't have many commentaries (and smaller ones often don't) ask if they have a catalogue or can tell you what is available. Checking the websites of various Christian publishers is also worthwhile.

Having used a commentary in preparation, don't just regurgitate what you have read but try to present it in a way that will be helpful to the group. Don't simply tell them what the passage means, but ask questions in such a way that you draw out what they think it is saying. This will help in two ways: first, everyone will feel valued that their view is worth hearing, and second, it will show you if they have really understood or are going off at a tangent. It is as important to plan suitable questions as it is to do the background study in the first place. Don't assume that because you have understood something, the rest of the group will.

If you prefer commentaries from the 16th and 17th centuries, you have a particular obligation to relate the study to life today, and to the theological issues being wrestled with in our culture. These issues are generally quite different from those of the Reformation and the period of the English Civil War. Some aspects of theology have remained unchanged for 2000 years, but many of the moral issues being wrestled with today (such as genetic engineering) were simply not known in those writings. Don't try to speak (and some people do this!) in the style of that era. For example, theology was often written quite aggressively, with plenty of dire warnings about judgment on those who disagreed. God's judgment should still be a very real part of our theology today and we shouldn't compromise to please our culture, but to speak in those terms (which often went beyond scripture) will make it look ridiculous. However, there are some aspects of theology often overlooked today which are dealt with in older commentaries, so they are not without value—but they do need to be used carefully. Try to balance their views by comparing them to modern ones.

You should resist the urge to give your group 'detail overload'. Some study leaders can get quite carried away by what they are learning from the commentaries and can assume that everyone wants as much detail as possible. This is likely to be boring and will not necessarily help the group relate theology to their lives and faith.

## SYSTEMATIC THEOLOGY

A systematic theology is one of the most useful books to have available if you are going to lead a Bible study. As the name suggests, this covers theology systematically; in other words, it covers each subject—God, Jesus, life after death, angels, and so on—looking at the relevant Bible verses and considering the various schools of thought on the subject. Even if you don't agree with the author's conclusions, a good systematic theology will have fairly covered all the alternative explanations as well. This is especially helpful with those subjects where there is a range of possible views, such as the end of the world. This sort of resource will give you more confidence to face possible questions although do remember that theology cannot always be neatly tied up; there are often loose ends and unanswerable questions that we simply have to live with. One of the best volumes currently available is *Systematic Theology* by Wayne Grudem (IVP, 1994). He deals with contemporary theological issues and generally presents alternative interpretations fairly. Not all systematic theologies are as helpful so be careful before you spend a lot of money!

## CONCORDANCES

A concordance is a book that lists all the major words in the Bible, telling you where they can be found. So, for example, if you want to find a particular verse but can only remember a few words from it, all you need to do is look up one of those words. All the verses in which that word appears are listed, and you can then find the one you want. This can save an enormous amount of time when preparing a study because you can look up all the verses on a particular subject in one go. Even if you know your way around your Bible, there will be times when you just can't remember the location of a certain verse. Two words of warning: if you do not have an exhaustive concordance (that is, one including every word) you may often find that the verse you are looking for isn't there. Second, you must use a concordance designed for the Bible version you use. If you are using the New International Version it is no good trying to use an old Authorized Version concordance that you bought cheap at a car boot sale. While the meaning is often the same, the words used are not, and a concordance works by the words used.

## BIBLE DICTIONARY

This is a dictionary of words found in the Bible. It is different from a concordance in that it works just like a normal dictionary, giving the meaning of the words rather than their location in the Bible. The only words in it, however, are biblical ones. Usually the dictionary gives the technical meaning of the word, and also examines the theology around that particular word. So the entry on 'justification', for example, would be a long one, explaining not just what the word means but its significance theologically. This can be very useful if you have no theological background as you can ensure you know what all the words mean in a particular chapter of the Bible before you start the study. Often Christians don't know what a word means but are reluctant to ask. A Bible dictionary means you can find out without embarrassment.

## DICTIONARY OF THEOLOGY

A dictionary of theology works in much the same way but it is not limited to biblical words. Theological terms not found in scripture (for example 'Calvinism' and 'Arminianism') are also included. It is unlikely that this would be needed in an average study, since most people don't use such theological terms, but may be a useful resource for background reading.

## GREEK AND HEBREW INTERLINEAR BIBLE

As you study particular passages, you may want to refer to a particular word in the Greek or Hebrew but don't know enough of these languages to be really confident. An interlinear Bible has the Greek and Hebrew written directly above the English translation. This can be helpful for identifying the ways in which particular words are translated at key points. Unless you are very good at these languages an interlinear Bible will be more useful than a straightforward Greek or Hebrew version.

## QUESTIONS PEOPLE ASK

People are generally very predictable and they nearly always ask the same questions. If you are able to answer these questions with some degree of competence it will build trust and they will accept more readily that there are some questions you cannot answer.

It is important to assess the motive behind questions. Some people may ask because they are searching and they raise issues that are real hindrances to their believing. Others are confused on a certain point and hope you can clarify it for them. Some non-Christians, however, do not want to believe and are asking questions to try and find a reason not to do so. They may be hoping to catch you out. This is not a new tactic. The Pharisees did it to Jesus (Matthew 22:15–22 and Luke 20:1–8), so you are in good company! Then there are those who will listen to the answer (and who therefore can be reached) and those who, no matter what you say, still argue the point. An indicator of the latter attitude is that they ask another question on a different topic almost before you have got your answer out. So, for example, they may ask a question about evolution and as soon as you answer they then jump to suffering or some other issue, rather than engaging with the original subject. It can be helpful to point out gently to someone like this what it is they are doing and to refuse to answer more than a certain number of questions each time. For some people no answer will be convincing enough because they just do not want to know. They fear the implications for their lives if Christianity turns out to be true.

It is unlikely that you will set out to do a whole study on these predictable questions, especially if you are using a printed study course. They tend to come up in the discussions around various theological issues or Bible passages.

Below are some of the most frequently raised questions and some outline answers. It is not within the scope of this book to answer each question fully—after all, some of these issues have not been resolved in two thousand years of church history and so are unlikely to be definitively answered in your study group! The answers given here are only outlines but they also include certain principles that may be more helpful for the individual concerned than a full theological summary. Where appropriate particular books will be recommended if this will help with further study. The aim of this section is to point you in the right direction for thinking through what the answers could be. Many people do not want complex, theological responses to their questions—they simply want to know that Christians have thought about this issue and that there is at least some kind of answer. Some of them are the questions that would be asked in an evangelistic study rather than one for believers, but there are many believers who are disturbed by some of these issues but are afraid to ask in case they look as if they are doubting or suffering a spiritual crisis.

## 1. IF GOD IS A GOD OF LOVE, WHY IS THERE SUFFERING IN THE WORLD?

This has to be the number one most frequently asked question. Incredibly, many Christians have never thought it through, especially those who have grown up in a Christian family and may not have had to wrestle with this subject themselves.

It is important to try to establish if the question relates to personal suffering rather than the philosophical question in its general form. If you think it may be related to personal suffering then you should take a much gentler approach rather than just treating it as an issue for discussion. You may need to spend time talking through the personal issue before dealing with the broader question. For most people, however, it is not personalized, although they can sometimes get emotional about what they have seen on the television.

There is no single answer to the question of suffering but certain aspects of the issue can be explained to help make more sense of the whole. The first is, of course, that the human race is in rebellion against God. If people obeyed the teaching of the Bible most suffering would end. Much of it is directly attributable to human selfishness. This is where non-Christians tend to want to have their cake and eat it. They don't want God to control their lives (if they did, they would be Christians) but they don't want to take responsibility for their actions either. They want to be able to sin and avoid all its harmful consequences. This is neither desirable nor possible.

Suffering also has a purpose in alerting us to the fact that all is not well in our relationship with God. It shows us something is wrong, just as pain in the body tells us we have injured ourselves. When we see suffering it should make us question what is wrong with the world and that in turn may make us seek God for an answer. C.S. Lewis described suffering as 'God's megaphone'. In other words, when things go wrong the Lord is able to get our attention away from our day-to-day pleasure-seeking existence and encourage us to consider eternal issues . Many people are saying to God, in effect, 'I'm going to ignore you and defy you, but when I'm in trouble I expect you to rescue me and if you don't I will blame you for the trouble I'm in.' This attitude doesn't need answering—it needs exposing!

Some people will accept human responsibility for some suffering but will raise the issue of natural disasters. Surely God must be to blame for these? Many so-called natural disasters can be directly traced to human activity. Deforestation in Nepal results in flooding in Bangladesh or India. Pollution caused by human greed results in the depletion of the ozone layer, or the greenhouse effect. Not all natural disasters have an obvious cause, but even with these the Bible points us to an explanation. The apostle Paul says in Romans 8:20–23 that the whole of creation is in bondage to decay. The sinful rebellion of the human race means that we are not fulfilling the purpose God originally intended for us, and this has affected the whole created order. It will not finally be put right until the Lord creates a new heaven and a new earth (2 Peter 3:13).

None of these answers finally and totally resolves the issue, and it is important to acknowledge that in the discussion. It may also be useful, in an evangelistic situation, to ask the questioner what their answer is to suffering and in what ways it helps to leave God out of the picture. If anything, it makes the situation seem even more bleak. Two particularly helpful books on this subject are *Where Is God When It Hurts?* by Philip Yancey

(Marshall Pickering, 1991) and *How Long, O Lord?* by D.A. Carson (IVP, 1990).

## 2. HOW CAN GOD BE FAIR AND SEND PEOPLE TO HELL?

Many people wrestle with this question because of relatives or friends who have died without coming to know God, and others because they seem so ineffective in their evangelistic efforts. While some parts of the Church deny that hell exists at all and claim that everyone gets to heaven, this does not convince many people. There is a sense even among unbelievers that some people deserve to go there (Hitler and other obviously evil people are usually given as examples) and that it would be unjust for everyone to be saved. It is hard to believe that the Lord Jesus would have spent so much of his time warning about something that wasn't ever going to happen. At the very least it seems to suggest he was misleading people by what he said (see, for example, Matthew 5:27–30; Matthew 13:36–43; Luke 12:42–48; Luke 16:19–31) if in the end everyone gets to heaven. An excellent book on the subject is *Crucial Questions about Hell* by Ajith Fernando (Kingsway, 1991).

Three things need to be emphasized when dealing with this difficult topic. First, God is both a fair and loving Judge. He will take every aspect of people's circumstances into account when judging them. Genesis 18:25 assures us that the Lord will be just and absolutely fair in what he does. All of us tend to be harsher on those we don't like and easier on those we do, but God will judge fairly. It is also important to remember that our idea of right and wrong is very imperfect and the things we would overlook on the grounds that 'everybody does it' will not be overlooked by the Lord. It is his standard of right and wrong that matters, not ours.

Second, no one ends up in hell by accident. God is working towards our salvation long before we are even thinking about it. He knows when the best time is for us to respond to the gospel. No one will be condemned because they couldn't quite understand the sermon or because they were killed the day before attending an evangelistic meeting. The Lord will ensure that all those who can be saved will be reached in some way (John 6:37–40).

Third, in a very real sense people send themselves to hell. The most famous verse in the Bible, John 3:16, tells us that God sent his Son into the world because of his love for it. Verse 17 says, 'For God did not send his Son into the world to condemn the world, but to save the world through him' (NIV). Those who finally end up in hell have turned away from a God who wanted to save them. They have refused his mercy and his offer of forgiveness and that is why they are punished for their sin.

Within our culture of blaming other people and never taking responsibility for our actions the idea of being held accountable by God may come as a shock to some. We mustn't go beyond scripture with lurid accounts of people burning in fire, but at the same time we must not deny what Jesus taught just to please our cultural sensibilities.

### 3. SURELY THE BIBLE HAS BEEN CHANGED, LIKE 'CHINESE WHISPERS'?

Many people don't understand how the Bible came down to us. They think of the old whispering game and assume that the Bible text has changed just as much as any other message passed on over the centuries. For seekers this can be an obstacle to faith, since they may feel they cannot trust what the Bible says. Some Christians may also find this a problem and they may feel they have to believe in the Bible as an act of blind faith, as deep down they doubt that it really is reliable. A key problem here is that people often misunderstand the way the text was transmitted and translated. Many people think that each new translation is a revision of the previous one, in a linear sequence like this:

Hebrew — Greek — Latin — King James — Revised Version — New International Version

If that were the case, they would have very good grounds for doubting the Bible's reliability. But it didn't happen that way. Each time the translators went back to the original Hebrew and Greek and did not merely update the previous edition.

In thinking through the issues surrounding the reliability of the Bible you need to consider what is meant by 'inspiration'. Sadly, some Christians may dogmatically state things that are simply not true and which to an informed person can seem plainly ridiculous. An example of this would be the statement, 'This Bible is word-for-word what the apostles wrote.' That is obviously not true, partly, of course, because the apostles themselves did not write much of the Bible! It is also technically not true because what we have is a translation, so it cannot be word-for-word what the original author wrote.

More important, however, is the fact that (as the footnotes of most Bibles make clear) there are variations in the manuscripts. So how can the reliability of the Bible be upheld if there are variations in the manuscripts? You need to remember several key factors here. First, all the variations are minor and do not affect any major Christian doctrine. If the deity of Christ, for example, was only found in the uncertain verses, then that would be a major concern. But this is not the case and neither is it for any other central doctrine. This is important because the idea is often put about that Jesus was just a philosophical carpenter who became a God-like figure much later on as the stories about him were exaggerated. If that was the case the manuscript differences would occur in the verses where his deity is revealed—but they do not. In fact, the absence of variants at key points in the manuscripts means that we can have even greater confidence in the factual basis and reliable transmission of the teachings at the very heart of the Christian faith.

Second, there is such a large number of manuscripts available that errors can be identified and eliminated. It would be impossible for all the copyists to have independently made the same error at the same point in the same book of the Bible. In fact the errors are usually obvious and only found in a minority of manuscripts, or in much later ones.

Third, it is interesting to note that when the Gnostics (a second-century heretical group) appeared, they did not feel free to change the existing four Gospels but instead wrote their own books. Within 50 or so years of the Gospels being written, they knew that they couldn't merely add their ideas to them and get away with it. This shows that there wasn't the second-century 'free-for-all' of scripture alteration that some non-Christians claim.

It is also interesting that many parts of the Gospels that were frankly embarrassing and inconvenient for the early Church remain unchanged. If they had felt free to alter the record, they would have most certainly altered these parts. So, for example, the risen Lord Jesus appears first to women (Matthew 28:9–10). In the first century, women were considered to be very unreliable witnesses, prone to emotion and hysteria. To have them as the first people to see the risen Lord seriously undermined the credibility of the claim that he was risen from the dead. Why is it in there? It can only be because it is true and no one felt at liberty to alter it.

Some Christians get confused because they have the same view of the Bible as Muslims have of the Qu'ran. Muslims believe that each actual word of the Qu'ran is given by Allah in Arabic and that the Qu'ran is perfect and there can be no other versions of it. They believe that the Qu'ran cannot be translated because each word is important, and they therefore quite consistently claim that it should be read in the original to be fully comprehended. Mohammed played no part in the transmission of the Qu'ran, apart from reciting it. Christians, however, believe that the writers of the Bible were inspired by God and guided by the Holy Spirit, who used their personality, experience and culture to produce the final work. The human authors of the Bible were not mere robots, but played a part in the writing. The final result was what God intended but he did not simply overrule the human element. The Bible can and must be translated so that people around the world can fully understand it. The issue is not primarily that of the actual words, but of the truth they convey.

There is a vast range of books on the subject of the reliability of the Bible and examining the issues of historical reliability and how the text came to us. Anything by F.F. Bruce is always worth reading. Craig Blomberg has also written two very helpful books, *The Historical Reliability of the Gospels* (IVP, 1987), and more recently *Jesus and the Gospels* (Apollos, 1997).

## 4. SURELY THE BIBLE IS OUT OF DATE?

Some people (including some who would call themselves Christians) accept that the original authors were inspired by God but say that things have changed greatly since it was written and so it cannot be fully relevant to life today. In short, it is out of date. Obviously it is true that the examples and illustrations of the Bible are describing a world very different from the one you or your study group grew up in, and these need careful application to our own situation and circumstances. The central issues of the Bible, however, are God, human nature and how the human race is reconciled to God. None of these things has changed a bit. The Bible's descriptions of human nature could have been written yesterday. And the more humorous ones, such Proverbs 27:14—'If a man loudly blesses his neighbour early in the morning, it will be taken as a curse'—seem very relevant! As you study the Bible its amazing relevance to life will become apparent, and that's the best way to answer this particular question.


## 5. DON'T ALL RELIGIONS LEAD TO GOD?

This is an extremely common view in today's culture. It seems very tolerant and nice to say that all religious people (some add, 'if they are sincere') will find their way to God. In many cases those who say this are simply showing their utter lack of understanding about the various religions and their teaching. Simply describing some of the differences can help them to see how ridiculous this statement is. Muslims teach that Jesus was not the Son of God and that he did not die on the cross. Christians teach the exact opposite. There is simply no way both can be right.

Some would say it is incredibly arrogant to say that your belief is right and everyone else is wrong. In fact it is the one saying that all faiths are right who is arrogant. They are claiming an insight greater than that of all the religious teachers of history. In a sense they are claiming the ultimate revelation of all time—that all religions lead to God and all the founders of those faiths were quite wrong when they said they didn't.

A question linked to this is that of the eternal destiny

of those who have never heard the gospel. Until recently, those of other faiths lived in distant lands and it was easy to assume dismissively that they were all doomed. Today, however, people of other faiths live all around us and it seems to many that mission work has failed since there are more Hindus, Muslims and Buddhists in the world today than ever before. How can God condemn them when they have not heard the gospel?

This is a difficult area, not helped by the harshness of some on the extreme wing of evangelicalism, who discredit the biblical position by their unloving attitude. They may carelessly talk about 'millions condemned to a lost eternity', yet have never lifted a finger to advance the gospel overseas. This is very different attitude from that of the apostle Paul who spoke of his 'great sorrow and unceasing anguish' for those in Israel who had not responded to the gospel (Romans 9:1–3; 10:1).

This is an area where again we need to be reminded that God is just. He will not condemn someone for not believing a message they have never heard. That would be plainly wrong. What the Bible does make clear is that God will judge people on the basis of the knowledge they had. Everyone can see a created world around them and therefore can know there is a creator (Romans 1:20). No one can claim to be totally unaware of this. In Luke 12:47–48 Jesus uses the parable of the wise servant to illustrate the point that judgment is directly related to opportunity. 'That servant who knows his master's will and does not get ready or does not do what his master wants will be beaten with many blows. But the one who does not know and does things deserving punishment will be beaten with few blows. From everyone who has been given much, much will be demanded.'

Although we can be reassured that God is just, it is no good thinking those of other religions are all right as they are. There is still a very real urgency about taking the gospel to the world around us. Other faiths have religious teachers, they do not have a Saviour. Obviously this must be done in true humility and with a willingness to hear other people's viewpoints.

## 6. DIDN'T THE DEAD SEA SCROLLS DISCREDIT THE BIBLE?

Probably more nonsense has been written about the Dead Sea Scrolls than about any other archaeological find. These scrolls were found in 1947–48 in caves near the Dead Sea. Many scholars believe that they were the sacred books of a Jewish sect known as the Essenes. Some were books of the Old Testament, others were the writings of the Essenes giving directions for how to live in their community, and describing their beliefs, especially regarding the end of the world.

Most people know nothing about them but have a vague sense of unease that they are somehow a problem for Bible-believing Christians. In fact the scrolls confirm much about the reliability of the Old Testament and say nothing to undermine the New. Some sensationalist paperbacks claim that the Roman Catholic church realized the scrolls disproved the Christian faith and so hid them to make sure that no one (apart from the surprisingly well-informed author of that particular book) would know what they said. It is worth noting that since all the scrolls have now been published, the conspiracy theorists have gone very quiet. Where is the shocking revelation that the Church was trying to hide? The publishing of the last of the scrolls has largely stopped the wild theories, but for some people it may still be an issue.

A very helpful book for those who want to know more about the Dead Sea Scrolls but don't have time to plough through the thousands of publications on the subject is *The Dead Sea Scrolls Today* by J. Vanderkam (SPCK, 1994). A book like this can be useful if any of the members of your group have been influenced by some of the many sensationalist books that have come out over recent years. Although they may have no academic credibility, these sorts of books can influence those who don't know much of the Bible or early church history, and can cause unnecessary doubt.

With all the resources available, no one should feel that they don't know enough to lead a Bible study. It will take commitment in terms of time, and you may have to think through some hard issues, but in the end you will find that your own faith benefits from this study as much as the faith of those in the group you lead.

If particular areas cause you difficulty do talk to someone in your church leadership. If they don't know (and ministers are not omniscient!) they may well be able to point you in the right direction.

There will inevitably be the odd occasion when someone raises a question you have never thought of, let alone have the answer to. In those (hopefully rare) cases you should be honest, admit you don't know and promise to find an answer and come back to them with it in the near future. Make sure you do. People don't mind waiting for an answer, but they do expect you to come back to them after your research.

The more you lead studies the more your understanding and confidence will grow and you will wonder why you never thought to do it before.


## SELF-ASSESSMENT BIBLE QUIZ

Still not sure you know enough? Try this test to assess your Bible knowledge. Answers are given on pages 58–59, but don't cheat and look them up! The way to assess your results is given afte the answers.

### Q.1
In which books of the Bible do the following characters appear? (1 point for each)

a) Rebekah        b) Samson        c) Darius
d) Cornelius      e) Onesimus

### Q.2
What was the result of the building of the Tower of Babel? (1 point)

**Q.3**
Name the only two men sent to explore the Promised Land who didn't die of a plague. (1 point each)

**Q.4**
Who built the first temple in Jerusalem? (1 point)

**Q.5**
Who was in charge of the successful rebuilding of Jerusalem after the exile? (1 point)

**Q.6**
Name one of Job's three friends. (2 points)

**Q.7**
Which prophet saw a valley of dry bones? (1 point)

**Q.8**
What does *Eloi, Eloi, lama sabachthani* mean? (2 points)

**Q.9**
Which prophet had an adulterous wife? (1 point)

**Q.10**
Which Gospel describes the visit of the Magi? (1 point)

**Q.11**
Apart from the resurrection of the Lord Jesus, which is the only miracle to appear in all four Gospels? (2 points)

**Q.12**

Who was High Priest the year Jesus was crucified? (1 point)

**Q.13**

Which two New Testament letters would you study for the theme of justification by faith? (2 points)

**Q.14**

Where is the apostle Paul's clearest writing on the resurrection (book and chapter)? (2 points)

**Q.15**

Where did John receive the visions described in the book of Revelation? (1 point)

## ANSWERS

1.  a) Genesis    b) Judges    c) Daniel
    d) Acts    e) Philemon
2.  God confused languages
3.  Joshua and Caleb
4.  Solomon
5.  Nehemiah
6.  Eliphaz, Bildad and Zophar
7.  Ezekiel
8.  'My God, my God, why have you forsaken me?'
9.  Hosea
10. Matthew
11. Feeding of the five thousand
12. Caiaphas

13.  Romans and Galatians
14.  1 Corinthians 15
15.  Island of Patmos

## SCORING

**21–25 points**: You have a good overall knowledge of the Bible. Don't be complacent, but you should be able to lead a Bible study.

**16–21 points**: Not bad, but you would find it helpful to do some background reading before undertaking the leading of a group.

**5–16 points**: You should spend some time reading (see list of aids to Bible study) but don't give up!

**5 points or less**: Have you *ever* read the Bible? Don't even think about leading a study until you have!

# CHAPTER 3

# EVANGELISTIC STUDIES

John had spoken to Dave, his neighbour, on many occasions about his faith, but Dave had never seemed interested —until now. Since being made redundant, Dave had been doing some hard thinking about the goals in his life. As the conversation developed, John could see how open Dave was; but where did he go from here? Should he ring his minister and ask him to visit? John wasn't sure his minister would be able to relate to Dave. Should he invite him to church one Sunday? But then John thought about the services, and he wasn't sure Dave would like them. What could he do?

This is arguably the most important type of study for small groups or one-to-one situations. Many Christians can identify with the scenario above where a contact is made and someone is open to hearing more, but there doesn't seem to be a clear way forward.

## WHY NOT JUST ASK THE CHURCH MINISTER TO VISIT?

This may be a good idea—but not always. First, many ministers are simply too busy, and if they are able to visit, it is not likely to be very often or very soon. This can leave the contact with a lot of unanswered questions as it usually takes a lot more than one visit to work through all the issues relating to faith. If they are rushed through a discussion they may well feel they are just being told to believe it, rather than coming to those conclusions themselves.

Second, many ministers are trained and gifted to care pastorally for believers; that is what they are called to do. This does not necessarily equip them to speak to seekers about the basics of the Christian message. They may get too technical and simply not make sense. The Bible clearly describes various roles within the leadership of the Church (Ephesians 4:11–13) and clearly distinguishes between an evangelist (one who brings the gospel to those outside the Church) and the pastor (one who teaches and cares for those inside the Church). Unfortunately many Western churches still operate on the 'priest can do it all' principle, which is not only unbiblical but also unfair. Few ministers are prepared to admit their gifting does not include evangelism, but it is rare for someone to be gifted both pastorally and evangelistically. If you do feel it is right to ask your minister to visit then make sure you go as well, at least for the first visit, so that you can introduce the minister and 'break the ice'.

It is also important to remember that relationship plays a key part in a contact such as this. There has to be trust, particularly as the issues being touched upon affect the deepest and most personal aspects of someone's life. That trust does not come quickly or easily.

The contact is very unlikely to know the minister, but they do know you. They may well find it easier to trust you than someone they have only met once or twice before. There may also be some resistance from the non-Christian if they see the minister as a professional 'selling the gospel' to try and keep the church going. When it is a layman talking to them, however, they are much less likely to suspect their motives.

## WHY NOT JUST INVITE THEM TO A SUNDAY SERVICE AT CHURCH?

It can be hard for a Christian used to going to church to understand just what it means for a total outsider to go to a service for the first time. Many non-Christians would be very nervous about the idea of going to a church service. It is simply too great an unknown quantity. They don't know what will happen or what they will be asked to do. Will they be asked to stand up and say something? Supposing they stand up or sit down at the wrong time? All these concerns can seem very trivial to an established Christian, but to the seeker they are important issues. No one likes to look a fool because they don't know what they are doing and that is often the unbeliever's concern. Few people under 40 ever went to Sunday school, and so apart from weddings and funerals (which are not always in a church either) they may never have been inside a church. One reason why an outsider is more likely to go to a Christmas service than any other is that they have a much clearer idea

what will happen, maybe through attending carol services at school.

If the church is not part of a well-known denomination—Church of England, Roman Catholic or whatever—they may also have concerns about it being a cult
and the danger of brainwashing. These concerns are not
helped by sensationalist media stories and soap opera
plots about people being kidnapped by cranky religious
groups and having their minds taken over.

At the opposite end of the spectrum people may not
want to go to church because they view it as boring and
irrelevant. Many people's image of church is a handful
of hat-wearing old ladies sitting in a dingy building,
warbling along to a mournful hymn. This image is often
confirmed by the media, and maybe even by a visit to a
church in the past. They will not be able to connect it
in any way to their lives and the circles in which they
move. It's the spiritual equivalent of anorak-wearing
trainspotters (with apologies to all trainspotters!) The
unbelievers just do not think church has anything that
would attract them. The problem here is that they have
confused the church with the Christian faith. Being able
to do a Bible study first and find out about the life and
teaching of Jesus may help to overcome the negative
image that they have. It will mean that they can begin to
distinguish between what the Bible teaches about the
Christian life and what some churches practise.

Also, the church service will almost certainly be unsuitable for a non-Christian. Many aspects of the service (especially if it's Communion) will seem downright
bizarre. Singing hymns or songs, and especially praying,

are things that may put off many non-Christians from coming again. The focus of the Sunday service is usually on encouraging and teaching believers, and even so-called evangelistic services may be more focused on the needs of the church members, and what they will or won't find acceptable, than on the concerns of the visitors. Routine parts of the service, such as the collection, can also be a problem since a visitor may get the impression that they have to pay to be there and that the underlying issue (which they always suspected) is for the church to get money.

Unless your church is very well set up for seekers and sensitive to their needs, it can all too often give the impression that church is a strange subculture which excludes the visitor. Evangelism is, in effect, saying to the unbeliever, 'You can be like us.' If you and the people at your church are the only Christians they know, and you are inviting them to become a Christian, they will interpret that as becoming like you. That can be very attractive if they see a Christ-like life being lived out before them, and the community of the people of God caring for one another. This was certainly the situation in the early church in Jerusalem (Acts 2:42–47). They made a real impact in the city because people could see that the faith made a positive difference. Few churches in the Western world offer such examples of community, even though it would be a powerful witness in our fractured society. Sadly, what outsiders may in reality see is a subculture a million miles away from what they know or are used to, and that they don't find it inherently attractive. They may feel that church is a place to which they could never bring their friends and that they could never be like the other members.

All these issues can combine to put them off ever coming again. If the seeker has first done a series of studies, however, not only may they have come to faith themselves, but all the issues relating to churchgoing can be discussed and worked through. It may be that the church itself has lessons to learn from the new-comer's observations of its practices. Going to a one-to-one or small group study can then lead to attending church at a later date, and time can be given to talking through what actually happens in a service and what will be expected of them. Make sure you cover even mundane issues like what to wear and where to sit. If your church is particularly culturally sharp they could produce a video of a typical Sunday service so that those in the study group could watch first to get a clearer idea what they were going into. This could then be talked through and any strange aspects of it explained. The video should reflect a normal Sunday and not some one-off special event at which Billy Graham preached and Cliff Richard sang! If the gulf between the video and reality is too great, they may feel they have been conned. Building a relationship with people through a study group means that when they do start to go to church you can 'debrief' them after the service (since ideally the studies will be continuing) and talk through anything that put them off or that they didn't understand.

Another problem with church services is that they are very unlikely to deal with the particular questions the seeker has. Most church services assume that all the basic faith questions have been dealt with and focus on the implications of the Christian faith in this or that area of life. Unbelievers often want to know about UFOs or Nostradamus or reincarnation. Not many churches are likely to have a sermon on the possibility of alien life forms visiting this world. Another issue of vital importance in most people's lives is that of sex and relationships. Few ministers are brave enough to preach directly on sexual issues (even though the Bible has no such inhibitions!), and this can give the impression that the Christian faith has nothing to say on such things, but only deals with 'spiritual' matters. Unanswered questions in this area more than any other can result in enquirers giving up on Christianity. In a one-to-one or small group study you can encourage people to ask questions on any topic and then (perhaps with a little research) find some answers.

Encourage group members to keep a notebook with their Bible in which they write down all the questions that occur to them during the week. These questions may be prompted by a TV programme, a comment a friend made, a difficult passage they read in the Bible. If they don't write the questions down, they may forget them and will be frustrated by a nagging sense of something not being answered. You may need to come back to them with an answer, so make sure you write the question down as well so that you remember! Many unbelievers ask the same questions and some of the most frequent were dealt with in Chapter 2. This can be a starting point for your research. Many Christians find their own faith has been greatly strengthened by dealing with these issues and clarifying for themselves what they really believe and why.


## MIND YOUR LANGUAGE!

I am not suggesting here that you are likely to break into expletives during the study (I hope). I am referring to the much more important issue of avoiding Christian words, phrases and initials which the non-Christian will simply not understand. This is crucial, because it is very unlikely that they will say anything about it. No one likes to look a fool so people will simply nod and pretend they know exactly what you are talking about. I once visited a man who was very keen on computers and who was enthusing about his latest purchase. At the time I knew nothing about computers (and know very little now!) but spent the evening hearing about twin hard drives, RAM and ROM and, reluctant to admit my ignorance, I simply made the right noises at the right points interjecting the occasional 'Really?' when his tone of voice implied I should be impressed. I left him not having understood a word, but with my host quite unaware of this. Sadly, the same can happen in an evangelistic study. The visitor will not openly admit their confusion but will give the impression that it is all being enthusiastically taken in, while in fact they don't know what you have been talking about.

Study leaders must resolve to eradicate all religious language from their vocabulary or, where it cannot be avoided, to give an explanation immediately, whether their hearers have asked for one or not. Take time to make up your own list of the religious words you use most often and think of easily understandable alternatives; then work hard to use them. The most frequently used words will vary depending on your denomination. Every church has its 'in' language—which should be banned in evangelistic studies!

Anyone with a grasp of theology will realize that not all the substitute words on your list will have exactly the same meaning as the word they are replacing. This does not matter, because in an evangelistic study you are communicating the basics of the Christian faith, not a comprehensive theology. Of course doctrine is important; it defines how we understand God and his working in our lives, but it should not be the starting point for the new enquirer. Obviously the presentation of the basics must not be so vague that it gives a misleading picture of the Christian faith. People must be clear on what it is they are responding to; but for many Christians saying too little is not the problem!

Another thing to avoid is using illustrations and examples from the Bible and church history that the enquirer will not know. It may come as a shock to some believers that many people have no idea who John Wesley or Martin Luther or Cardinal Newman were, so examples from their lives are not likely to create much impression. Similarly, references to Abraham and Isaac or Ruth and her 'kinsman redeemer' will only cause confusion. Probably the only Old Testament characters you could refer to would be Noah and Jonah! It is much more effective (and more biblical) to use everyday things and situations as your examples in the studies. In the Gospels Jesus constantly illustrated his points with everyday examples such as sowers and their seed, gathering harvest in, sheep and their shepherd and so on. The apostle Paul did the same when in Athens (Acts 17:22–31). He realized that the people there didn't know the Old Testament so he didn't refer to it, instead he used creation and Greek poetry to make his point.

Sadly, many Christians have little idea of what goes on in the world because for years they have been shut away in the semi-monastic world of church meetings. If you are to lead an evangelistic study well, you will need a general grasp of issues in the news and in ordinary life. You don't need to devote all your time to trying to live as a non-Christian but you should have some idea who is who in sport, politics, music and films. This can be invaluable for finding illustrations to communicate to the enquirer. The apostle Paul must have taken time to read Greek poetry to be able to quote it, and we need to take a little time simply to know what is going on in our world.

It may be worth going through your chosen study course first, looking at the points made and trying to think of illustrations that will clarify them. Some people find this sort of thing very easy, others may need to give it more time, but it is a key part of the study and should not be neglected. It is also worthwhile collecting quotes and anecdotes (especially from famous people) that illustrate important aspects of life.

As you spend time with your group members (or member) it may be obvious that some aspect of the

Christian faith or life concerns them particularly. This can range from believing in miracles to what changes they will have to make in their own lives if they are to follow Christ. If you suspect one of these areas is of particular concern to a member of your group confronting them about it directly may not always be helpful, particularly if it is a more personal area such as sexual relationships. Instead, try to voice the question for them and say something like, 'Some people have a problem with this because...' Go on to give the answer without directly asking them if it includes them. That way, if you are wrong it doesn't matter and if you were right (but they wouldn't want to admit it), you are still dealing with the issue but without putting them on the spot.

It can often be helpful to admit your own struggles in coming to faith—what you found hard to believe or to obey. Obviously some discretion may be needed if you are referring to past sins, but generally people find it more helpful to know that you have been through the same difficulties rather than viewing you as 'super-spiritual', or somebody who has never been tempted or doubted in their life. But make sure that you don't allow the study to become an opportunity for telling all your favourite stories about yourself, and be very clear in your mind what the point of each illustration really is! What they may especially want to know is how your faith helped in that situation. Admitting you are still there may rather undermine their confidence that the Christian faith can help them improve or grow!

If you use anyone else as an example it is best to be

vague or change the details so that the person cannot be identified—or even merge several examples. The world can be an amazingly small place and it would be very damaging if, halfway through the illustration, they realize that they know the person concerned. It is best to tell them that all examples are anonymous and composites of several situations, otherwise they may fear they too will become one of your examples in a future study.

As people begin to grow in faith they may find they have difficult personal issues that they need to raise with you—moral dilemmas, requests for advice or confession of sin. Make sure you think about how to handle these situations before they arise. It is especially important to have someone to whom you are accountable as a study group leader and with whom you can talk through any particularly difficult problems that arise. Ideally this should be your minister or an elder in your church, someone who has had experience of dealing with seekers or the newly converted and the problems they have to deal with as they seek to follow the Lord. In terms of confidentiality you may need to tell the enquirer that you will seek advice from your minister, but that it will go no further. Most people can accept this, especially if they can be assured of the minister's trustworthiness and that he will not in turn tell someone else within the church. It is important that evangelistic studies are not done by 'lone rangers' in isolation from a church and with no accountability. That can so easily lead to all sorts of problems and misunderstandings.

# WHAT ARE THE ESSENTIAL ELEMENTS
# OF AN EVANGELISTIC STUDY?

We said earlier that the aim was not the teaching of all doctrine, but rather to focus on the essential elements. There has to be enough content for people to understand how to become a Christian and what the basic implications of that decision will be for their everyday lives. Different churches may have a slightly different emphasis in these areas but a certain minimum can be described as 'non-negotiable'.

## SIN

First, people need an awareness of their sin and the need for forgiveness. We are all different and for some this will have a very real and immediate aspect; for others it is an awareness that grows on them the more they grow in faith. This is a non-negotiable, however it is realized. If there is no sin that needs forgiving, then why did Jesus go to the cross? The central theme of Christianity —the human race being reconciled to a holy God— ends up as something of a non-event. This emphasis does receive criticism, and some would say that we need to help people feel good about themselves. That is undoubtedly the message of our self-obsessed culture, it is not the message of the New Testament. From the very first sermon (Acts 2:36–40) through the letters of the apostles, to the book of Revelation, the message is clear: the human race has been separated from God by its rebellion. Obviously if you are talking to someone who is suffering from depression or some form of self-hatred, you should avoid focusing on sin until they have first been reassured of God's love for them. In the end, though, it cannot be ignored.

On the other hand, it is important not to go to the opposite extreme. Don't denounce your group as sinners at every study! Some people feel that the impact of their teaching is directly proportional to the volume with which they speak, and they find an urge to raise their voice every time they deal with the subject of sin. Even more bizarrely, some feel that sin can only really be dealt with by talking in Elizabethan English, furnishing their denunciation with quotes from the King James Version of the Bible. This will almost certainly be counter-productive. Jesus made it clear in his teaching that it is the Holy Spirit who convicts people of sin and their need for righteousness (John 16:8). Trying to force people to feel guilty is wrong and a sign of a lack of trust in the Holy Spirit to do his work. In the end such teaching is nothing more than manipulation, something unworthy of the name Christian.

Apart from a few brash personalities, however, most Christians are more likely to hold back from dealing with the question of sin than they are to overdo it. Another advantage of a pre-set study course is that the issue can be covered without group members feeling 'got at' because they can see it is a study that everyone does. There would be no implication that they especially need to know about sin! It is important to make clear that we are all sinful, including you as group leader, otherwise you can be seen as self-righteous.

## GOD

It may sound ludicrously self-evident that a study about the Christian faith should include something about who God is. The very fact it is so obvious, however, can be the problem. According to all the surveys, about 65 per cent of the UK population say they believe in God. A closer examination reveals that for many it is an empty word and they are really quite muddled about what they think constitutes the deity in which they claim to trust. You should give time to asking the enquirer what they understand by the word 'God' and then introduce them to some of the qualities and definitions of God from a Christian perspective. If this isn't dealt with at the start, it can create all sorts of problems for their faith later on because they continue to have a misleading picture of the Lord. When speaking to people in this sort of situation in Athens, the apostle Paul began with a basic outline of God as Creator, the source of all life, someone who cannot be likened to anything material and the one to whom we will all give account one day (Acts 17:22–31).

## JESUS

People certainly need to understand who Jesus is. Many think of him as no more than a good man or as some sort of persecuted prophet figure. Your studies would have to make clear that he is much more than this, that he is the Son of God, the second person of the Trinity. Jesus himself stressed that the issue of his identity was key to understanding and responding to the gospel (John 8:24). This can be quite a difficult subject and you may need to give more time to it than is allowed for by the study course you are using. This doesn't matter. This is such a crucial area that it is worth making sure those in the study group have really grasped it. Some may find the idea of Jesus as the Son of God easy enough, it is relating him to the Trinity that many struggle with, but you cannot deal with the question of Jesus' identity without covering the Trinity also. Think beforehand about illustrations you could use to help explain this. Sadly, many Christians don't think about these things and when they are asked to explain what they believe, they are at a loss. While such concepts are, of course, beyond our full understanding, it is not good enough simply to dismiss them as a 'mystery', if that is just an excuse to avoid thinking! It would be worth listing some of the Bible verses that point to a triune God. There isn't a single 'proof text' that you can use, but rather a range of verses that together point to the identity of Jesus as God. Do keep a spare copy of a helpful book or booklet on this subject, that you can lend out for reading between the studies and discuss afterwards. Alistair McGrath's superb book *Understanding the Trinity* (Kingsway, 1990) is a good place to start.

Sadly, many Western Christians have a poor grasp of early church history, when Church Councils wrestled with the Christian understanding of God as three in one. In taking someone through a study on the person of Jesus it may be helpful to have a copy of the Athanasian Creed (found in the Book of Common Prayer) to give them, not to memorize it (generations have done that without understanding a word), but to use it as a framework for explaining what the Trinity is and is not.

## THE SIGNIFICANCE OF JESUS' DEATH AND RESURRECTION

Historically, various denominations have emphasized different aspects of the cross, and their Bible study courses reflect this. What is important is that those doing the study are clear at a basic level what the death of Jesus achieved and what makes his resurrection so important. Unless the person studying with you has just finished a degree in philosophy, they will probably not be helped by an in-depth analysis of all the possible theological implications of the cross. It is hard for some Christians to accept the importance of simplicity; they feel that using simple language fails to reflect the incredible nature of what was achieved on the cross. While there is certainly a time for more complex theology later on, as somebody grows in faith, all they need to know initially is that they can be forgiven for their sin and reconciled to God through Jesus' death on the cross, when he took the punishment for their sin upon himself in a supreme act of love and sacrifice.

The most helpful area to emphasize in regard to the resurrection is its historical reality and its implications for the claims of Jesus, who himself made his resurrection the proof of his claims (see Matthew 12:38–42 and John 2:18–22). The fact of the resurrection and the evidence for it can be enormously helpful in establishing Jesus' unique authority and showing that the Christian faith is not just a nice idea but is actually grounded in history. In a culture influenced at least to some degree by post-modernism, such evidence can be crucial in showing that the facts are true in an ultimate sense, not merely true for you.

## THE BIBLE AS THE WORD OF GOD

Reasons for trusting in the reliability of the Bible were set out in Chapter 2. I would like to stress, though, the need to encourage people to experience for themselves the Bible as the word of God. It is one thing to be convinced at an academic level of the historical accuracy of a manuscript, thanks to the latest archaeological discoveries; it is quite another to engage with it meaningfully day by day. Explain how the Lord has spoken to you through personal Bible reading. It may be appropriate to buy some daily Bible reading notes and to ask for feedback on how the reading is progressing. Christian bookshops usually have a range of materials ranging from CWR's *Every Day with Jesus* to *New Daylight* published by BRF. *Word for Today*, published by UCB, is another very popular one. Encourage group members to mark and highlight their Bibles as they study, and even to write personal notes from their reading. This can be helpful to look back on and remember what the Lord has said and the encouragements he has given.

## WHAT IT MEANS TO LIVE AS A CHRISTIAN

This is undoubtedly the most difficult yet vital area since there are so many and varied opinions about it within the Church. Some study courses include a section on this, many do not. Neglect it and you may leave unresolved issues that will hinder spiritual growth. Overdo it and you move from New Testament Christianity to a legalism bound to a particular subculture that either kills their interest or creates Pharisees (and the Church has plenty of those already).

Don't make the mistake of expecting instant perfection. Sometimes believers who have taken years to get their lives sorted out expect a new convert, just finishing the first study course, to have eliminated all sinful attitudes and actions from their life. People need to know that you (and more importantly God) still accept them in the midst of all their struggles. A condemning attitude is not only wrong, it will also drive a person away from the Lord. Sometimes the churches that talk loudest about the grace of God rarely exhibit it themselves.

## MAKE SURE THE STUDY IS AT THE APPROPRIATE LEVEL

Just as people vary in their spiritual responses, so they also vary in their academic ability. Some will want a course that wrestles in detail with the text and its meaning. They will love discussing subtle points and will feel confident to share their views or opinions. Others will want a much more simple approach, clarifying the basics and not giving too much detail. There is a wide range of material available and it is very important to match the right material to the ability of the individual or group. Do not simply use the material you like or can teach easily. In fact it may be best to let your group choose by showing them several options. Problems may arise if one person in the group finds the course too easy or too hard. Where there is a very obvious difference in ability try not to include both in the same group. While it would be right to expect believers to work through issues together and still accept each other, many enquirers may feel less patient or be more easily put off.

## DON'T PRESS FOR A RESPONSE TOO SOON

Some people will have been prepared by the Holy Spirit for the study and for them it will simply be a case of putting the pieces of the jigsaw together before they take a step of faith. Others may have something of a church background and will respond readily. Some, though, may have a lot of issues to work through and may not respond as quickly as you would like. It is vital not to put pressure on people to respond before they are ready.

This highlights an important aspect for the study leader. The purpose of the study is to help the individual or group to a living faith. There can be no room for pride in results, proving a point, looking impressive or whatever. Sometimes others in the church can make this worse by asking why the group members haven't responded yet, or pointing out that there is a baptismal or confirmation service (the ceremony may vary according to church—the pressure is the same!) coming up and it would be really good if the group were ready by then. The study leader must simply ignore this pressure. How each member of a group responds must be between them and the Lord, so long as they know how to make a response when they want to. So much damage can be done by rushing someone who is simply not ready to make a response. In this regard there may actually be a problem with the course material itself, as some courses assume a very quick response. This is certainly a criticism that has been made of the Alpha course. For somebody who already attends church but has not yet made a personal response, this may be fine. But it is unhelpful to ask someone with no church background, after just a few weeks of teaching, to respond to the gospel. If your material takes this approach, it is important to think in advance what you will do when you get to that point and they still haven't responded. With some courses the material is such that you simply carry on, regardless of the response (or lack of it). With others, however, the assumption for the rest of the course is that the person doing it has made a faith commitment and so subjects such as prayer can now be explored. How you deal with this will depend on your confidence as a study leader. Some may want to move from the pre-set course to further studies on basic issues. Others may want to go over those first studies again. In some circumstances it may be right to carry on and to use the subsequent material to explain what the

Christian life will be like. Usually people understand that they have not yet responded and that therefore some of the subjects are not applicable at this stage. It may be a good moment to ask them if they have any particular concerns that are holding them back from taking that step of responding in faith.

## DEALING WITH TANGENTS

A common problem in evangelistic studies is the tendency of group members to ask questions that take the study off at a tangent. Sometimes the question does have an obvious link with the theme under discussion and in these cases it isn't too much of a problem. The question can be answered and the issue explored without losing the thread of the main study. Indeed, as already mentioned, encouraging questions is a vital part of involvement and interaction within the study. At other times, however, the question is so tangential that it is impossible to link it in with the study and may well mean the theme for the day is lost.

Several factors can help assess whether this is worth going with or not. First, is it a habit? Does someone do this every week? They may not be aware they are doing it or understand how disruptive it can be, and simply pointing it out to them may be enough to resolve the problem. Second, is it an unanswered issue that is troubling them? Sometimes people keep going back to a subject because they either feel it hasn't really been dealt with or some aspect of it continues to trouble them. In these cases it is essential to try and identify the cause for concern and give time to dealing with it specifically. Finally, it might just be the way that particular person thinks, in which case you have to work with it. Some people just have to ask what pops into their heads. If it is really taking the studies off course it may be worth alternating week by week, between doing the preset study and working through all the questions that come up (that you have written down as they are asked). Balance must be maintained: the questioners should never feel that their concerns are being ignored or avoided, but the studies do need a structure if they are not to become repetitive and focused just on various members' needs.

## HOW LONG SHOULD THE STUDY LAST?

As long as it takes! It is best for people to continue in a study group for at least a year after they come to a real faith. The study material will, of course, change to something more appropriate for believers. A year may seem a long time but many people go through various crises of belief in their first year and the study group is a good place for them to talk it all through. There are many statistics to show that a horrifyingly large number of people fall away from the Christian faith after making a response to the gospel. One of the key factors in my experience has been the lack of someone to turn to while they are in the early stages. New converts need support, encouragement and the knowledge that they are not alone. Someone who has been a Christian for years will have developed ways of coping with doubt, temptation and disillusionment. New believers will not have these coping mechanisms and need to be supported, in their first year in particular. In an ideal situation they will then be ready for training to lead a study themselves.

The study material used after people come to faith will need to cover certain key areas. It may be appropriate to look at doctrine in more detail. Now that they understand the basics of the Christian message, you can spend time exploring with them other secondary areas of doctrine. You will also need to help the person explore how they will explain to others what has happened to them. This can be especially important where immediate family and friends are concerned. People often worry if someone they know 'goes religious' and they may see it as their duty to rescue this person and to get them back to normality. If the new convert has been given an opportunity to talk through how he will explain what has happened to him and how to present the gospel to others, it will give him much greater confidence. All being well, it should not only reassure friends and family but will catch their interest so that they too will want to join a study group.

It is also crucial to help new believers find their role in the church. Some have claimed that if someone doesn't have a role in a church within eighteen months, they will leave. New believers can find themselves very much on the fringe of church life, welcome to turn up to anything but never asked to do anything. It would be

important in your studies to look at the biblical picture
of the Church as the body of Christ (1 Corinthians 12),
and to emphasize that everyone's role is important, not
just those in a leadership role. Help them to think about
what their role and gifting may be. After a year or so,
when they have become more settled in their faith, it
may be helpful to work through their SHAPE with them.
This looks at:

**S**piritual gifts: What gifts has the Lord given them?

**H**eart's desire: What do they have a particular concern
for or interest in?

**A**bilities: What are they particularly good at, able
to do well?

**P**ersonality: What sort of personality are they? Does
that fit with a particular role?

**E**xperience: Has their life experience prepared them
for something particular?

The aim of working through this checklist with someone is to help them to see if there are particular things
they may be able to do within the church fellowship. It
is a serious mistake to assume that because someone is
fairly new to the Christian faith they must sit on the
sidelines for 20 years while they mature. People mature
best in their faith by being active. Obviously there need
to be safeguards and some guidance given, but not to
the extent of excluding them from any meaningful part
in church life.

There will obviously come a point when the study
group can end, but even then for a few months after-

wards, you will find it helpful to keep in contact with your group members and ensure all is well. It is better to devote time to a few people who really then grow in their faith than to rush through thousands who just fall away.

Sadly, some will not want to continue with the studies and will not come to faith, and this has to be respected. Real damage could be done by being too pushy. Sometimes at a later date people may want to pick it up again and this can be done if you have maintained a harmonious relationship with them.

Evangelistic studies offer a very real way for the 'average' Christian to share their faith effectively with those around them. All things considered, they are an opportunity not to be missed.

# CHAPTER 4

# EXPLORING THE BIBLE
# AS A FAMILY

The couple were young and so in love. He gazed at her, she at him. 'Darling,' he murmured. 'There's something I want to ask you.' 'Then ask,' she replied expectantly. Hesitantly he said, 'Could we study Deuteronomy together tonight?'

Many Christians experience the strange but common phenomenon that the hardest people to pray and study with are one's own family. Time and again families set out with the best of intentions but find that somehow what works well with other believers just doesn't work in a family situation. It is difficult to be quite sure what the cause is. No doubt a large part of it is a feeling of artificiality. Trying to be 'spiritual' with someone who knows you so well can easily seem contrived. There can also be a sense of embarrassment that is hard to overcome. Whatever the reason, the sad result is that many couples and many families do not pray or study the Bible together at all.

## DOES IT MATTER?

Many (perhaps most) families do not pray and study together and yet seem to do very well spiritually, so does it really matter? If they are fine not doing it (and maybe that's true for you), is there really a need to start? This argument can be a little like saying that Great Aunt Hilda smoked 40 cigarettes a day, every day from the age of 12 and lived until she was 102. Therefore I can also smoke and it won't affect me.

People often confuse regular church attendance and involvement in church activities with spiritual growth and development. One may involve the other but they are not the same thing. There are people in our churches who are 'running on empty'. They are still busy, they still go to the meetings, but for them the reality has gone. Times of family Bible study cannot be a guaranteed protection against that but may go some way to helping, because some aspects of a family study simply cannot be duplicated anywhere else. There is also the simple fact that because this kind of study involves other people, it is more likely to happen. We may resolve to pray or study on our own but if other things come up that resolve can be quickly forgotten. If, on the other hand, we have prearranged a time to meet and study with other members of the family, we will feel a certain sense of obligation to be there, and a sense of positive pressure to spend time studying instead of watching television!

The Lord has put all of us in some kind of family and many of his commandments are to do with protecting family life (see, for example, Exodus 20:12, 14). This is not just because family life has enormous social benefits, but also because it can be a means of spiritual encouragement and growth. One of the most important aspects of a family study is that there can be no false spirituality. There is an atmosphere of reality based on very intimate knowledge that simply cannot be reproduced in any other context. No one on earth knows us as well as our families, and that means that we have to be honest in looking at the application of biblical teaching in our lives, in a way that might not happen in a church setting. It can be all too easy in a church Bible study to agree verbally with what is being taught, even if our own lives are far from it, since it is unlikely anyone will know the truth. In a family study, however, any gulf between belief and practice is much more readily noticed. The answer is not to avoid the family study but to allow it to challenge and change us.

For most Christians, going to church and attending mid-week meetings are a key part of the Christian life; family worship alone will not be a substitute. Study times within the family should not be used as an excuse for separation from the wider fellowship; that is unbiblical and unhealthy and could result in domination by one member of the family. The wider fellowship is needed to help avoid personal interpretations of scripture that are heretical. With no other guidance or input a family group could even begin to operate like a cult, with no one to challenge whatever bizarre teachings are dreamed up.

## BUT WE ARE ALL SO BUSY!

Time pressure is often the reason given for not studying and praying as a family. There is no doubt that for some people this could be a problem, but for many it is just an excuse because they find such study so hard to do. For others it may be a reflection of wrong priorities—somehow they always find time for their social lives and sporting activities. Obviously social and sporting events are an important part of family life and it would be ridiculous to argue that every spare minute has to be spent in Bible study, but the issue should not be one of either/or. The one-eyed, square-faced idol that sits in most of our lounges demands so much of our time in 'worship'. Perhaps a little less time could be given to watching TV and a little more to nurturing family spirituality. A recent study claimed to show that the brain is less active when a watching TV than when a person sits in an empty room doing nothing at all! Of course, some families are in difficult situations where pressure on time is a real issue and not just an excuse. In those circumstances the aim should be to seek to do a little study well. There must be one window in the week when the whole family is free. Make sure you identify and then guard that space!

The following sections look at different family situations and suggest ways for developing studies in each. The suggestions are not by any means comprehensive, and you may well think of your own, more appropriate to your immediate family circumstances. There is also a large degree of overlap. What would work well in one situation may well work in all of them.

## THE ENGAGED COUPLE

This may seem a strange place to start looking at the question of family Bible studies, but it is exactly where we should start so that habits are formed that will be carried into married life.

Most people's thoughts at this time are more of a dreamy, romantic nature and talking about Bible study can seem out of place—a little like this chapter's opening scenario. Somehow it doesn't seem to fit the romance novel setting. Obviously there is a lot more to being engaged than studying the Bible together, but for a Christian couple, omitting it totally would be a mistake. Taking time to study together brings a spiritual dimension to the relationship. Engaged couples are often reminded not to be so involved with each other that they forget their other friends, and this advice could be extended to 'don't forget your God'. The Lord needs to be at the centre of the couple's plans and relationship and studying the Bible together can help that.

Study can also give a couple the opportunity to talk through meaningful issues (such as what motivates them in life) and to get to know how the other one thinks and feels about a range of issues. They will get to know the real person better rather than just their carefully groomed social image. It is surprising how many couples can be together for a long time and still not really know the other's thoughts and beliefs on spiritual matters. A crucial part of Christian marriage is sharing the journey of faith together and for this to happen, the couple need to talk about it. They may even discover that they have differing views on quite important aspects of faith that will impact their married life. If that is the case, it is better to explore its implications before marriage, not after. It would be useful to take time to study and discuss aspects of biblical teaching that will apply to their life together, touching issues such as the roles of men and women, sexual relationships, bringing up children and so on.

Studying together can also help reveal underlying attitudes to matters like money or the possibility of full-time Christian work, which can be enormously influential in the success or otherwise of married life.


## HUSBAND AND WIFE

Many of the reasons for a husband and wife studying together are, of course, the same as for an engaged couple. As time goes on, however, people's thinking develops and changes as their understanding grows of how the Lord works in their lives. It is important as that thinking develops it is shared within the marriage, otherwise, ten years on, it can seem as if the couple have drifted apart spiritually and don't really know the person to whom they are married.

A time for study together also gives an opportunity to communicate and talk through life issues raised through the studies. This can be extremely important for couples who might not find it easy to talk about deeper matters. The aim of these studies is not in-depth theological analysis but rather applying scriptural principles to life. When such life issues do arise, part of the study time can be given to praying them through. It is surprising how many Christian couples fail to pray about problems that arise in their families. Maintaining a spiritual dynamic in a relationship is probably one of the hardest and yet most important things a couple can do.

There aren't many studies specifically designed for married couples, but more general ones can be just as useful, if you seek out ones that relate in some way to everyday situations. Bible editions prepared specifically for married couples can be useful as they contain some study and devotional material, applicable all through married life and not just at the beginning.

Make sure that you use time for studying together to study! There is a danger that busy couples who don't get much time simply to talk will use the study time for catching up. Such times of talking are crucially important in a marriage but if they replace the original purpose of looking at the Bible then they need to be reconsidered. Maybe extra time needs to be found to talk so that the study is kept as just that.


## STUDIES WITH CHILDREN

The Bible puts a great emphasis on the responsibility of believers to teach their children about the Lord. In Exodus 12:26 one of the reasons for the Passover festival was to teach the children about the events surrounding Israel's escape from Egypt, so that it would not be forgotten by subsequent generations. It was not just history that the people of Israel were to teach to the children, but also the Lord's commandment (Deuteronomy 4:9–10). Paul commends Timothy for his faith which he says has been taught him by his mother and grandmother (2 Timothy 1:5).

We may assume that parents will want to teach their children about their faith, yet very few actually do so at home. It is a mistake to rely solely on Sunday school. Most Sunday schools operate for about 30–40 minutes a week. The world has far longer each week to try to influence your child the other way! Studying together will not merely communicate factual information about who did what in biblical times, but will begin to give children a biblical worldview. This worldview will not become a reality for them until the Holy Spirit applies it to their hearts and minds, but parents can lay a vital foundation that will help counter the unceasing tide of consumerism and self-indulgence that characterizes our culture in the West. It would be foolish to underestimate the impact this has on even very young children. The MTV/soap opera culture is very effective, and it is nearly always anti-Christian. Think for a moment of all the most popular soap operas. Who are the Christian characters in them? They are probably one of three types— the self-righteous busybody, the well-meaning but incompetent fool, or the sinister manipulator. Christians are never presented as normal, trendy or the sort of people you would like to imitate. This constant anti-

Christian propaganda (for that is what it is) has a subtle negative influence. The answer is not to run away from the world, or to force this on your children, but rather to help them identify and cope with these influences.

Enthuse your children about discovering a biblical worldview by telling them you are all going to explore the Bible—that has a much more exciting feel to it than 'studying' the Bible. If the children come to think of the Bible as boring then they will begin to dread and resent reading it, the opposite of what you intended. Of course, all children have their difficult days when even the most exciting activity is declared 'boring', so don't panic unnecessarily, but if it's clear that Bible study really isn't communicating, then something may be wrong with your presentation. Try asking the children how they would like to do it. They may well think up some surprisingly creative ways.

Make Bible study interactive and relevant to the children. Many Christian bookshops have a wide range of children's activity books that can help you, and Sunday school materials can be an excellent resource. It would be best to choose different materials from those your church already use or you could run into problems with duplication. Publishers such as Scripture Union and BRF have a wide range of resources for use with children, both individuals and groups. Even simple things can help, like using a map of the Bible lands and looking up place names on it whenever they are mentioned in the text. Use video excerpts as part of your Bible exploration. So, for example, an episode from the life of Jesus could be read in one of the Gospels and then the same incident could be watched from one of the videos of Jesus' life. Two particularly good ones are *Jesus of Nazareth* and the animated film *The Miracle Maker*. For an Old Testament story the video series *Testament* would be good. There is also an increasing number of CD-ROMs available on many of these themes.

Aim to read the Bible together once or twice a week, and do it thoroughly, rather than having a compulsory time every day that simply causes stress. The days of a father sermonizing over the breakfast table as his children listened attentively are a world away from the pre-school rush that is most people's weekday experience. Make time for the Bible study so that it isn't preceded by shouting and screaming at the offspring to hurry up, resulting in anything but an atmosphere of spiritual calm.

Parents often over-estimate their own children's depth of spirituality. Up until the age of about 10 or 11 children tend to be naturally compliant and will want to please you. They will probably give you the answers you want to hear rather than ones that truly reflect what they are feeling or thinking. This isn't a problem where factual answers about Biblical geography are concerned, but what about when a response to the gospel is called for? Christian parents can be so keen (very understandably) for their children to respond in a positive way that the child begins to believe that his or her acceptance by the parent is dependent upon it. This can be disastrous for the child's spirituality in later life. Obviously some children do come to a very real faith at a young age, but many who 'make a commitment' at the age of eight have no idea what they are doing. They simply sense this is important to make Mummy and Daddy happy.

Teaching children in home Bible studies will need to be more than just sharing your favourite Old Testament stories and endless evangelistic presentations. Children need to connect what they read about in the Bible to their world and their life. They need to begin to see the wisdom of a biblical worldview and how it differs from the culture in which they live. None of this is easy, and it certainly can't be done in a hurry, but if the goal is clear, the route to it will become plain. Simply repeating the gospel message in its narrowest sense can be extremely damaging. You can end up making the gospel sound dull—a disastrous consequence! It is more effective to only explain the gospel message on an occasional basis and then really to emphasize it.

You need to be careful in dealing with the issue of judgment as far as children are concerned. Like everyone else, children need to understand what it is that the Lord Jesus saves us from, but an unbalanced emphasis on hell can create the image of a terrifying, tyrannical deity in their young minds, setting up a major barrier to the gospel in later life.

Make sure you use a Bible version that children will understand. The New Century version is excellent for children and young people. It is an actual translation (not a paraphrase) but uses accessible language, avoiding some of the potentially confusing words found in the NIV. A good example of this is the word 'aliens' (see for example, the NIV on Exodus 22:21). For children growing up watching *Star Trek* and *Roswell High*, aliens are from outer space. The New Century version uses the word 'foreigner', which is much less likely to cause confusion.

## SOME IMPORTANT DOS AND DON'TS

- If you have more than one child, don't make the study in any way competitive or overly applaud the child who gives the 'right' answers.
- Don't make it too much like school. Even if your children enjoy school they probably won't want more of it at home.
- Do spend time having fun with your children as well. Some Christian parents can be suffocatingly serious and spiritually paranoid. There is a time for a Bible study and a time to do something fun or just plain silly with the children.
- Don't rush children into praying prayers of commitment. If they really do seem ready, it may be the right step, but see it as part of a journey of growing in faith, not a one-off decision. Children rarely appreciate the full implications of becoming a Christian and too strong an emphasis on a 'once and for all' decision can hinder future spiritual growth.

## TEENAGERS

If children can generally be described as fairly compliant, the opposite is surely true of teenagers. Many parents would probably be tempted to abandon the idea of family Bible study when the children reach teenage years. Obviously by then persuasion rather than any form of compulsion is vital, but in many ways it is through the teenage years that young people need a guide they can rely on, and being shown how to use the Bible in that way could be very valuable.

The study will have to change from being explorative and taught by parent to child to being interactive and discussion-based. Teenagers want to feel that their views are being heard and respected. Nearly all teenagers assume it is a law of nature that they know more than their parents! While that may not be an attitude to encourage, it does mean that they will need to be involved in talking about the meaning of a passage and relating it to their lives and situation.

The aim of Bible study for children and teenagers should be to help them grow up seeing faith as an integral part of life. Teenagers have to face a range of issues on which it is possible to find clear biblical guidelines. In our culture the most obvious of these are money, alcohol, drugs and sexual relationships. It is vital that young people do not confuse the biblical view on these topics with the (perceived) restrictions set by parents. It may be that their parents' view and the Bible's coincide but they need to realize this themselves from their Bible study. They need to come to their own conclusions about what the scriptures teach and begin to understand why. Some parents may feel that the embarrassment level is just too high to look at issues like the Bible's view of sex, but often a teenager has questions and wants to know the reasons for the biblical perspective. However embarrassing it may be, it is a crucial area of communication, perhaps more easily done by one parent rather than both, in a one-to-one setting rather than in front of the whole family.

## USING FESTIVALS

As I have already mentioned, Exodus 12:26–42 describes how the Israelites were to use the Passover to remind their children of what the Lord had done for Israel in bringing them out of Egypt. Part of the purpose of the festival was to be a living illustration reminding them of the Lord's goodness. This was to continue in succeeding generations so that they did not forget the Lord. Using the major festivals in the Church's calendar as an opportunity to teach about different aspects of faith can be a valuable aid. Those from a non-conformist background might not be familiar with some of the festivals but virtually all churches acknowledge the major ones, such as Christmas, Easter and Pentecost.

Christmas and Easter are particularly good, and a biblical focus at these times of year is especially important, given the way that they have been hijacked by consumerism so that many in the West have only the vaguest understanding of their significance in the Christian calendar. Biblical teaching will also help children distinguish between the fantasy (Father Christmas and Easter bunnies) and the true meaning of these festivals.

## STUDIES WITH THE ELDERLY

If you are doing Bible study with elderly family members, you may well find that they fall into one of three categories: those with a living faith, those with no faith and those with what could be described as a nominal faith. Many older people grew up in a society where it really wasn't 'the done thing' to say you didn't believe in God. If you weren't convinced, you simply didn't practise it much beyond regular or occasional church-going. Of course, people rarely fit neatly into categories, but knowing where they are spiritually will affect the sort of study you do.

Members of your immediate family may find it hard to accept teaching or guidance from a younger member of the family. It isn't easy to overcome this but you should make every effort not to appear patronizing or as if you 'know it all'.

With those who have no faith, and who know they have no faith, what you are doing is an evangelistic study. You should bear two things in mind, however. First, do not assume that simply because they are older they are necessarily nearer death than you are! Some people feel they can justify being direct to the point of rudeness because the elderly relative could die soon and so they need to be told before it is too late how to find forgiveness and prepare for eternity. People are not converted by rudeness, no matter how well-intentioned. Second, if an older person begins to see the truth of the Christian message they may well begin to wrestle with feelings of regret over a wasted life. While they can be assured of forgiveness for all that was wrong in their life, realistically they will have limited opportunity now to serve the Lord. If they express this regret, allow them to talk it through, but help them to understand that God has used the whole of their lives to bring them to this point of faith and that it is the eternal reality before them that they should make their focus.

With those who are believers you can talk through what themes and subjects they would like to cover, from what they know (however much or little) of the Christian faith. For those who have a vague belief, but little idea of what the gospel is really about, you could do a series of studies on what it means to be a Christian, or look at biblical examples such as Cornelius in Acts 10, who was a God-fearer but didn't know the gospel. God had to send Peter to explain it to him. Using this example (or any others you can think of) you can gently challenge them to move on in their faith and gain a clearer understanding of what Jesus has done for them.


## STUDIES IN A DIVIDED FAMILY

This situation, where only one of the parents is a Christian, is potentially the most difficult context in which to do a family study, because there may well be disagreement as to the value of doing any Bible study at all. Generally, if your spouse is not a believer, try to involve them in some aspect of the social life of your church first, rather than leaping in with a Bible study.

Being involved socially will help them to meet other Christians which might dispel some of their fears and misconceptions about what it means to be a Christian. If they do want to find out more and to start studying the Bible, it is best to get someone else to help them. This may seem to contradict the advice at the beginning of the chapter about married couples studying together but it doesn't, because this is an evangelistic Bible study Someone outside the relationship will be less emotionally involved and no doubt less likely to be over-zealous in their evangelistic efforts. Some Christian spouses can be something of a liability when trying to convert their partners. They can so easily forget all the basic guidelines for evangelism—being subtle and giving space to the enquirer—and go for a high-pressure approach that is counterproductive. You may be able to do an evangelistic study together if the session is led by someone else, but check with your spouse first if they really want you to be there and don't be hurt and offended if they say no. Men especially can struggle with admitting their ignorance of the Christian faith in front of their wives.

The greatest problem will arise if your unbelieving spouse objects to you teaching the Bible to your children. This is an extremely difficult area. Naturally the believing parent will want the children to grow up knowing the Lord, but the first and most important thing is that the children are not used as pawns in the larger struggles within the relationship. Doing studies to try and score points is wrong. It is also wrong to use the children to try and evangelize the other parent, by getting them to say carefully scripted things to them. Some do this knowing that the other parent will be reluctant to hurt the child's feelings by dismissing what they have to say. If, however, the children quite naturally raise an issue relating to faith, that is fine: you shouldn't make embarrassed attempts to silence them or it will look as if you are teaching them something you don't want the other parent to know.

In most cases some sort of compromise can be worked out. A key factor will obviously be the age of the children. If they are old enough to make a decision about it, then the final decision could be left to them. Sometimes a Christian partner can give in too easily. They can be made to feel that they are forcing their beliefs on the children and that doing nothing is the neutral option. The problem is that doing nothing is not a neutral option. It is as much a statement of faith to say that God does not exist, or that we cannot know him if he does, as it is to say that we can know him. The unbeliever's perspective is every bit as biased as the Christian's. Christian parents have a right (and an obligation before God) to seek to pass on their faith to their children, and the believing parent should do just that. Don't resort to doing the study with the children in secret, telling them to deceive the other parent. This is not a good example for the children. You may prefer to do the study when your unbelieving spouse isn't there so that you don't provoke them—but do tell them what you are doing.

With prayer, patience and determination, a way forward can usually be found. It is important not to give up. It is also very important not to allow this to become the big issue in your life, dominating everything you pray and talk about. If a believer becomes unbalanced by this situation they will make it worse not better. Sometimes the best advert for the gospel in a family situation is the Christian acting normally!

Exploring the Bible with those we love can be hard, but I hope that the ideas in this chapter will encourage at least some to step out in faith and develop a part of their family life that may have been neglected for many years.

# CHAPTER 5

# STUDIES WITH BELIEVERS

It was not a good evening. Steven had turned up late on the night he was supposed to be leading the study. The subject was 'Interpreting the Book of Revelation' and it seemed that no one could agree on anything. Mr Lambert was adamant that Steven's view was heresy; John the youth leader was shouting him down; and young Clare couldn't find where Revelation was in her Bible. 'I bet it wasn't like this in the early Church!' said Steven to himself, as he tried to regain control of the group.

One of the more obvious reasons for having a Bible study is to help believers meet together to study God's word. In some ways this is easier to run than an evangelistic study because the group members share a starting point of faith. Some aspects, however, need careful consideration if the study is to work. There can be a very real danger of underestimating the issues that may arise specifically because it is a study among believers.

## KNOW WHAT THE GROUP IS FOR

In many cases a study with believers will be in the context of your church—you have been asked to lead a house group. This might seem to resolve the question of what the group is for, but in fact it doesn't. Different churches have different understandings of what they are trying to achieve through their house group system. For many it is a straightforward mid-week Bible study and prayer time. Others, however, may be moving towards a cell church structure, where the mid-week meeting is far more than just a Bible study, but rather is intended to function as a church in miniature. The focus of this chapter, however, is the more straightforward Bible study and prayer meeting. Other types of study, such as special interest groups, are explored in more detail further on in the chapter.

Make sure before you start that you are clear what the house group is for and what is expected of you as its leader. Discuss this with your church leaders if you feel unsure. If a group doesn't have a clear purpose it will be in very real danger of drifting, and there may be occasions when you have to remind the members of your group what you are meeting for.

## A TYPICAL STUDY GROUP

In an ideal world, everyone who came along would happily and harmoniously study the scriptures and would agree together on the clear meaning of the passage. Encouraged by the perfect unity of the group and total agreement on every issue, they would then go into the coming week with renewed faith.

Unfortunately the reality doesn't always match the

dream, and the opening scenario described at the beginning of this chapter is closer to the truth than we might sometimes like to admit. Christians are human and at times have some all-too-human characteristics! It is crucial for the effectiveness of the group and the study that some of these dynamics are identified and thought about.

The single most influential factor in any group (apart from the Holy Spirit) is the personalities of the members. All groups are different, but certain sorts of people do seem to appear with monotonous regularity. Below are listed some (admittedly exaggerated) personalities you might get turning up at your study group. The genders assigned to the various personalities are for illustrative purposes only! It is helpful to think beforehand how you would deal with the various challenges they represent. Any one of these more difficult personalities could be enormously influential (for good or bad) in the group and so being able to deal with them is a priority.

Often when things go wrong in a believers' study group, it isn't primarily the material discussed that is the problem, but the people discussing it! Some people are used to chairing meetings in their secular employment and so can handle the difficult personality types more easily. For many, however, leading a study group is the only time they really lead anything and so they feel intimidated before they start, especially when it comes to sorting out problems. Do remember that if your church minister or elders have asked you to lead they must feel you have some ability! There are some training resources available which your leaders might ask you to go through. Sometimes, however, ministers can leave a group leader to sink or swim. This is not intentional, it may simply be that they are distracted by many other pressures. If you are particularly concerned about how you would handle a situation, however, mention it to your minister first.

## MR DOCTRINE

This gentleman has an excellent knowledge of the Bible and often church history as well. He is very clear on what he believes and shows great concern if the views of others don't match his own. His focus is often to 'convert' Christians to his own particular theological persuasion. He may well have a pet topic, such as the place of Israel in eschatology (the end of the world, to you and me), or why the Authorized Version is the only valid Bible, or the evils of the European Union.

Bear in mind that there are advantages to having someone like this in the group. They can in fact be a very useful 'resource', able to remember where those key Bible verses are. The issue is whether or not they will allow the group to function as a group and not as a congregation gathered to listen to them. If they are willing to co-operate they can play a part in the study. Sometimes it can be helpful to involve them deliberately at the start of the session so that they feel they have had their say and then let the group move on. If they do try and dominate, it is best not to provoke a confrontation in the middle of the study, but talk to them at a separate point during the week. Sometimes there can be a problem if Mr Doctrine is a lot older in the faith or in years than you, as he may not take kindly to being corrected by someone younger. Always refuse to get drawn into a discussion on his pet topic. It is very unlikely that you will manage to change his mind and you may well find that he succeeds in confusing you. The issue is not his belief but his behaviour and the way he seeks to dominate and influence the group. Depending on the situation it may be that a compromise could help. Suggest that one week he could lead the group and explain his view. (This is only possible, of course, where the view he is supporting falls within the bounds of orthodox Christian belief.)

A particular danger to be aware of (but without becoming paranoid) is that some Mr Doctrines will try to establish a group within the group and create a small following for themselves, perhaps by playing on any disaffection some members may have. New believers and a certain sort of person who likes everything theological neatly sewn up may be attracted to his certainties.

Sadly, some Mr Doctrines cannot be reasoned with. They want it all their own way, and will insist on correcting everything that doesn't agree with their theological view. In that case it is not always possible or desirable to keep them in the group. Resist the urge to criticize their behaviour when discussing the situation with the rest of the group. You may need to explain why they are no longer coming to the meeting, but do this graciously and with the minimum amount of detail. Often the rest of the group will be only too well aware of the problem.

## MRS GOSSIP

This lady seems to know a lot about a lot of people and has a burning desire to share some of her knowledge with the group 'for prayer'. If someone is ill, Mrs Gossip leaves the group in no doubt about what is wrong, often giving graphic details about the symptoms, especially with more personal or embarrassing conditions. Sometimes she talks cryptically about being concerned for a particular person and hints that she knows something about them that the group might want to know. Mrs Gossip can easily fill a whole evening going into great detail about various people and all the obscure connections between them and someone in the church. Uninterrupted, she would leave no time for a study at all.

Gossip is not only time-consuming, it is clearly condemned in scripture (Romans 1:29–30). It may be that the person doing it is not really aware they are gossiping, but the person—and the whole group—needs to know that this will not be tolerated. Doing a study on the theme of the Bible's view of gossip may be one way of approaching the issue. Reminding the group from time to time that gossip is not acceptable may also help. In an extreme case it may be necessary to interrupt the person and to say that the group is not an appropriate place to discuss what she is talking about. If this does become necessary you must follow it up with a private discussion with the person concerned at a later date. Explain why you did it and encourage them to say if they felt hurt by your interruption. The aim is to help them overcome the problem, not drive them from the group.

## MR TANGENT AND HIS COUSIN MR BABBLE

These two can be a handful for any group leader. Their speciality is going off the subject and taking a long time to do so! Mr Tangent will often seem to answer a question, but in doing so will raise another issue and take the discussion away from its intended direction. Sometimes the tangents can be useful, raising side-issues that other people may also be concerned about, and so you will need discernment! On many occasions, however, the tangents will not be helpful. They may well include Mr Tangent's favourite stories about himself (which everyone has heard numerous times before) or complaints about problems he has or doctrinal questions that have absolutely nothing to do with the theme of the study that evening.

Mr Babble can be an even greater problem. He is as bad as Mr Tangent, except that his tangents don't even make sense. After five minutes no one in the group has the faintest idea what he is talking about or how it has any relevance to anything. Sometimes it may be because he genuinely doesn't understand and is waffling because he wants to contribute even though he doesn't have much worth contributing. In other cases, it may be that he sees himself as something of a prophet, with a very profound understanding of the scriptures. The fact that no one can understand him is clear evidence to him of how profound he is.

Unfortunately you can't deal with these two by simply asking that everyone keep their contributions brief. People who talk a lot and who go off at tangents rarely realize what they are doing. You can't ignore this problem either, because the study will really be held back if it is continually hijacked in this way, and other members of your group will get impatient with them.

There are two ways of dealing with Mr Babble. The first is to interrupt gently. Concentrate on what he is saying and after he has had a fair opportunity to speak, jump in when he pauses (it may only be a small pause) and pleasantly but firmly take back control again. Thank him for his insight and immediately ask if anyone else has any thoughts on that topic. This moves the focus away from you to the group. The second way is to see him on his own. Ask him how he is finding the group. Commend him for his enthusiasm in contributing to the discussion and then explain that you are keen for everyone to have a say. It is easier to approach it in this way than simply to tell someone that they talk nonsense. Don't visit anyone while you are feeling angry with them—you may well end up saying things you regret. If someone has annoyed you, wait until the irritation has faded before approaching them.

## MISS SHY

The problem with Miss Shy is not that she dominates the meeting but that often you don't even know she is there. She will sit quietly, often in an inconspicuous corner, and will be reluctant to contribute anything to the meeting at all. Many shy people are actually quite happy not to be the focus of attention and it would be wrong suddenly to throw a difficult theological conundrum her way and expect an instant answer. Try to involve quieter members gradually by asking them first of all to read a passage from the Bible. Ensure it is a short reading without lists of difficult Hebrew names. In fact it may be best to ring them during the week before and ask them, so that they can rehearse the reading before coming to the group. It also takes the element of surprise out of it. Their contribution may well be as valuable to the group as that of anyone else, so be careful not to overlook them just because they are quiet.

Remember that people can be shy for all sorts of reasons. Some are quiet by personality and even in a one-to-one situation don't have much to say. Others, however, would like to speak but feel their contribution would be of little value. These need special encouragement to contribute. Be aware that sometimes you as the leader of the group can make the problem worse by appearing too much of an expert when it comes to theology. This can intimidate those who, not having had the opportunity to prepare in the way you have, will be afraid of sounding silly compared to your seemingly vast knowledge. Too much praise from the group for your depth of theological insight is not a good sign. It is actually a warning (although they won't mean it in this way) that you are losing them. These studies are not opportunities for you to display the peacock feathers of knowledge but to equip the church members to interpret and apply biblical principles in their lives.

## MR ANSWER-ALL

This gentleman is to be commended for his enthusiasm. He is so keen to contribute to the study that he feels he must answer every question. It is actually irrelevant whether or not his answers are right. If he is allowed to dominate the group, no one else will get a look in. Often he is unaware of his little problem and even speaking to him outside the study may be of limited benefit. Mercifully his type is quite rare but if one appears in your group, the easiest way to cope is to ask specific people to answer questions, so that if he interrupts, you can gently point out that you asked someone else.

## THE PERSON WITH THE WRONG ANSWER

One situation that you need to handle carefully is when someone gives the wrong answer to a question. Two factors to bear in mind will be the degree of error in the answer and the frequency with which that person gets it wrong. An important principle to establish, however, is that wrong answers must be challenged in some way. This is necessary for two reasons. First, if the group members do not realize that it is the wrong answer and you approve it, you have misled them and they may go on believing that error. Second, if the group does realize it is wrong, and you don't say anything, it could seriously undermine your credibility as the study leader.

Obviously you don't want to humiliate the person giving the wrong answer either, so a difficult balance has to be maintained. If the error is only slight, it is easy to handle, as you can repeat their answer and just add in the slight corrective. If it is one of the confident members of the group who nearly always gets it right but hasn't on this occasion, you can probably tell them that it is incorrect without destroying their confidence. The worst situation is where the answer is completely wrong and it has been given by one of the least confident members of the group, who always seems to be giving incorrect answers. Try to find something in their answer that you can commend and link to the real answer. If you do have to tell them it's wrong, make sure you use phrases such as, 'A lot of people think that', to help avoid identifying the individual as getting it wrong. Another approach would be to thank them for their answer and then ask if anyone can add anything, so that the correct answer can be presented without having to spell out that the first one was wrong. It may be that the material you are using for the group is just too hard for some members so if some people are consistently coming up with the wrong answers the material may be at fault.

## WHAT DO YOU STUDY?

If you are leading a church house group, this question will probably be answered for you by the leadership of the church. In most cases the leaders will encourage all the groups to study the same material, whether it is a pre-printed study or a Lent course or something they have designed especially for the church. There may the occasional week when it is left to the group leader to decide but it is unlikely that this will be the norm.

If your group has grown up around a special interest, then that interest will obviously influence the material you use. The group may seek to train people in evangelism or want to look at specific theological issues, such as the gifts of the Holy Spirit. Such groups can be valuable, although it is vital that they do not begin to think of themselves as superior to the 'average' believer and end up a divisive element in a larger church. Accordingly, it is probably best that a special interest group has a predetermined and limited lifespan. It would not be healthy for a small group to become too focused on a particular doctrine, as in time this could feed a sense of self-righteousness in the members and could result in a distorted theology, where the particular interest of the group is seen as the benchmark of spirituality and even, in extreme cases, the proof of salvation. In a normal group this cannot happen because most Christians have different pet topics and so they tend to balance each other out. The tendency for special interest groups to be divisive will be greatly exaggerated if no members of the church leadership are present.

## GROUP RESOURCES

There is a bewildering array of Bible study materials available, constantly changing as new material comes out. Most Christian bookshops should be able to advise you as to what there is and what would be most suitable for your particular group's needs. As the leader, you have the responsibility of selecting the material—so do so carefully.

There are several golden rules to remember when choosing this sort of material.

- Always go through it thoroughly yourself before deciding to use it in the group. This seems a hassle and an unnecessary burden on an already busy time schedule but its importance cannot be overstated. Material that may seem really good on the first page can change to being less suitable further on. If you don't know the material it will become obvious during the study. You may find that you give a full answer to the first question and, in doing so, answer the third and fourth questions at the same time. It may be that a very difficult issue is raised that you will want time to think about and to read up on before everyone starts asking if you agree with what has just been said! Failing to go through the material beforehand is a short cut too many. Preparing properly must be seen as an integral part of your responsibility as group leader. It may also help the group if you can recommend particular books to read if they have questions arising from the subjects being considered.

- Make sure the content is something that will really benefit the group. Resist the urge to study just what you like. If your church leaves it to each group to set its own studies then talk to the group about the sort of theological areas and topics they would like to consider. You don't have to follow every suggestion, but it would help guide you as to the issues that are of concern to them. It can be helpful to cover all the usual biblical and doctrinal issues and also occasionally to relate the study to world events. This can play a crucial part in helping the group see that Bible reading and study are not remote, isolated, theoretical exercises but that the issues dealt with do relate to everyday life. If a particular tragedy has taken place you could look at what the Bible says about suffering. If controversy has flared over genetic engineering or abortion or the environment, then these could become themes for the evening. This approach will also help the group members in their evangelistic witness in the workplace and with neighbours. If there is a particular issue in the news, friends and family will sometimes ask what the Christian view is.

• The material must be at the right academic level for the group, especially bearing in mind those who would perhaps struggle a little with complex theological concepts. It doesn't mean everything has to be ridiculously simple but it does mean you need to give time to explaining key theological words if they come up.

Sometimes it is best simply to study a page of the Bible and look at its meaning, context and application without lots of preset study guides. This can help the members of the group learn the basic approaches to what is called hermeneutics or how the Bible is interpreted. They can see how a text needs to be related to its context and look at issues such as the type of literature, the author's intent and so on. The leader of the group would have to do a lot more preparation for this but it could be more beneficial for the group in the long run. If every believer understood the basic principles for biblical interpretation, not only would they get a lot more out of their personal Bible reading but they would also be less vulnerable to some of the weird and wacky ideas that appear in the Church from time to time.

## WORSHIP OR THE WORD?

One factor that is sometimes controversial for a study group is the degree to which it involves worship. Some churches may think it inappropriate to have an act of worship without their minister or elder present. Others might say that the purpose of a study group is to study the Bible and not to 'waste time' singing songs. Yet others would claim that worship is an essential preparation for coming to the scriptures, in order to study them in the right frame of mind.

If you do decide to include a time of worship, you should consider several things. First, is the group ready for it? Worship in a small group is by its very nature an intimate experience. If the group is newly formed they may not feel ready to do something like that. It may take a few weeks for people to feel settled before worship can be introduced. Second, if you are planning sung worship, are there enough people with enough ability to make it a pleasant experience? Some will say that the most important thing is that we worship from the heart, and that is absolutely true, but anyone who has sat in a small group so musically inept that the resulting cacophony is painful to hear, will know that quality cannot be replaced entirely by enthusiasm. If musical talent is lacking, however, it doesn't mean the group cannot worship. Reading a psalm or a worshipful piece of scripture, or even reading the words of a hymn or chorus, and reflecting on their meaning, are possible alternatives. Sharing testimonies and answers to prayer can also be very encouraging. The group members may themselves have suggestions about what they could do.

## APPLYING THE TRUTH

Always remember that the studies are far more than academic exercises in looking at ancient Near Eastern documents. Biblical truths are supposed to change people's lives. You may like to have a time of quiet after the study for worship and reflection on what has been discussed, so that members can respond there and then if the Holy Spirit has been speaking to them. Occasionally, you could lead a prayer time that seeks to make the theme of the evening a reality in the daily experience of the group members. This models the idea that reading the Bible and studying it are supposed to result in changed lives, not just learning more information. This will be something people can take away and apply in their personal Bible reading.

# WHEN IS A GROUP A CROWD?

The dynamic of a study is greatly affected by the number of people present. Generally there are three sizes of group, based on the assumption that the meeting is being held in an average three-bedroom semi.

## FEWER THAN TEN

This is counted as a small group since it is quite likely that two of those present are the householders hosting the evening. A small group is not a problem if all members are there, but in reality some of the group will often be absent. This can be for a range of reasons—illness, holidays, other commitments or family crisis. If some of the group have young children then usually only one of the couple will be there anyway. As a result, the group that theoretically has eight or nine members may find that on average it has only three or four turning up on any given evening. This can be discouraging and may result in those who do turn up feeling that the group has in some way 'failed'. It can also discourage the leader if he or she has spent a lot of time preparing the study for only a few people. The leader may also worry that it in some way reflects on the quality of the studies, or that people are not finding them helpful. A general atmosphere of disappointment and failure can in turn result in fewer people still and the circle of decline sets in. This would be less of a problem in a very small church because there wouldn't be the expectation of a larger number in the first place.

There are also advantages to being a smaller group, of course, such as giving people the confidence to speak, but overall too small a group is in danger of having a negative effect.

## MORE THAN TWENTY

Various problems are created if the group is allowed to grow to this size, the most immediate being the venue. You may have a church member with a house large enough to cater for such a large group, but most do not, and so the pressure on the room available can become a very real issue. A crowd of people in a small space is tolerable for a few weeks. It may even be fun or encouraging, but people will eventually get fed up with it and start to stay away.

Another problem with allowing the group to become too large is that a lot of people will feel too intimidated to say anything. Limits on time would also prevent a lot of the group from contributing. If twenty people speak for just three minutes each, an hour of the evening has gone! Other more mundane factors are also affected by the group being too large. Serving refreshments can take an inordinate amount of time, with even getting the requests for teas, coffees and squashes becoming a feat of logistical skill. And how many homes have twenty mugs available?

## BETWEEN TEN AND TWENTY

This really is the ideal size for a group—big enough to cope with a few absences but small enough to be manageable. All the disadvantages described above are avoided and, if numbers are nearer ten, there is scope for growth. If they are nearer twenty, then thought needs to be given as to how to manage and control further growth.

If the group does grow and thrive strongly, it is vital not to make an all-too-common mistake and simply divide the group in half. Sadly this often results in both new groups struggling. A study group develops a certain dynamic based on the relationships of the people who attend. If it starts to get too big, dividing it in half will destroy those links that make the group what it is— everyone will have to start again and all sorts of problems and bad feeling can be generated. The key is to act before the group has got too big, when it is just reaching capacity. Then take a couple of people from the old group and use them to start a new group to which all subsequent new people are sent. This means the old group maintains its dynamic because the relationships are intact and the new group develops and grows on its own. It is tragic that this factor is so often overlooked and a really effective group is destroyed in the vain effort to multiply it.

If a group is declining, it may not be right simply to send more people to it. First, make a careful assessment as to why the group has lost members. It may simply be that one or two have died or moved away, or moved to another church. In those situations you should bring in new people fairly soon, especially if the number is starting to drop below ten. It may be, however, that it isn't the membership of the group that is dropping but the attendance, and this is a strong indicator that all is not well. Visit those who no longer attend and talk with them about why they have stopped coming. Bear in mind that their first answer may not be the real one! They may be trying to avoid hurting your feelings as group leader. If you think this is the case, ask your minister or elder to visit on your behalf. Another approach is to verbalize what you think the problem may be. Speak generally about 'some people' who think the studies are too long, too dull, or, whatever you think needs discussing openly.

Accepting criticism is never easy and it is important to avoid the two extremes of being defensive on the one hand and the 'I hate myself, I'm useless' mentality on the other. It may be that you feel the criticisms aren't justified at all, in which case you need to move ahead with seeking to enlarge the group. Probably at this point, however, you will need the input of an honest friend who may be able to help you assess more realistically what is going on. Sometimes it is not only group members who are blind to their faults and personality quirks! If you feel discouraged and wonder if you are up to leading a group after all then it would be best to speak to your minister or elder.

## GROUP VERSUS CHURCH

One reason why some church leaders are wary of small study groups existing in their congregation is the fear that they will be out of their control and may even result in dissent and insurrection. While that is unusual, it can nonetheless happen. Splits within churches are never good. Admittedly, they may subsequently be used by God, but there are many better ways to manage change. Jesus said that it would be the love believers have for each other that would convince the world we were his disciples (John 13:35), which may go some way to explaining our evangelistic ineffectiveness. Group leaders need to be loyal to their fellowship. This doesn't mean unquestioningly toeing the 'party line', but it does mean being willing to accept one's church and work with it despite its failings. If you are not sure of your commitment to your present fellowship then for Christ's sake (literally and reverently) don't lead a group. That is not the setting to work through any doubts you may be having about the direction your church is going.

You may find, however, that it is others who start to raise criticisms and questions. There may be those who will go beyond the occasional grumble about having drums in the worship service or the new liturgy, and actually seek to undermine the church leadership systematically. If this begins to happen, make it clear that the study group is not the place for raising these sorts of problems, and say it in front of the group. If you meet troublemakers on their own, they may accuse you of threatening them into silence. It is not a question of protecting the leadership or taking sides; it is simply that the study group is not the right place for such a discussion. This is especially so since the church leader isn't there to present his side of the story, which may drastically affect people's opinions (Proverbs 18:17).

Criticism may in fact be a symptom of a much deeper crisis in someone's faith. They may be struggling with discouragement or disillusionment with the church and may not be fully aware of this. If you feel you can understand or identify with their disillusionment (and it is something most Christians go through at some stage or another) then you may be able to help them by seeing them on their own. Relate your experience (in as much detail as you feel is appropriate) and get them to talk through how they are feeling. It is essential that you emphasize to them that doubt and discouragement are not sins. The Lord did not condemn Elijah (1 Kings 19) or John the Baptist (Matthew 11:1–11) when they felt discouraged, and he will not condemn them.

Leading studies with believers can be a real privilege, as we see Christians move on and grow in their faith and fulfil their potential in Christ. The rewards far outweigh the challenges that may also come along.

# IT ALL COMES TOGETHER

It had been a tiring evening, Peter thought to himself, but a very encouraging one. The group had made Sue, a newcomer, very welcome. Shy David had read the Bible passage beautifully and was obviously very pleased to contribute; and the discussion had gone so well. They had really wrestled with the topic and gone home with new ideas. Leading this group could be hard work sometimes, he reflected, but nights like tonight made it all worthwhile.

You may be at the stage of wondering whether or not to lead a one-to-one or small group study. You may know someone who would accept an invitation to an evangelistic study. Maybe you can see a real need for some believers at your church who struggle in their faith. Whatever the opportunity, it has to be worth exploring.

Many Christians go through their lives with unrealized potential. They feel they could do more for God but don't know how. Helping someone find faith in Jesus or really grow in their understanding of what God has done for them, or be motivated to serve the Lord in a new way is so rewarding. And it is something anyone can do—it is something you can do. You will have to work hard, preparing studies, visiting group members and so on. You will be discouraged at times, but it is a worthwhile task to set yourself. Many of Jesus' parables tell us that the things that count for eternity are very different from the things we so often focus on getting. Can you think of a better way of spending your time?